American Odyssey

A Collection of Bi-Polar Binges

By Buck Cochran

2013

Introduction by G.H. Coleman Jr.

Anyone can write stories about hell-raising in their youth. Some can write about their sordid journeys into adulthood. But no one can put a collection of these type stories together like Buck Cochran. He entertains you with stories that at times seem unimaginable, yet they are all so very true. All of his stories have the yin and yang of humor, and the sadness that goes along with having a mental illness.

But don't feel sorry for Buck, he is a survivor, and he never gives up! I told him several years ago, that he needed to write it all down….. It was all too important to be lost. The ingenuity, creativeness, and perseverance that goes along with each story is incredible.

The greatest part about being out and about with Buck, is that a simple night out can usually escalate to the event of a lifetime. Most people might be lucky if they ever see two or three of these type events. With Buck, it is an almost everyday occurrence.

Everyone has to confront their Demons, and when they do, some people lay down and give up on life. Others find a way to transform, and rise up out of the ashes.
This is a book about transformation, rising up, and surviving.

Enjoy reading this book. It proves there is hope for us all!

Table Of Contents

Rock Concert Story

One Friday night during the time that I was working at the plant (K-25) for British Nuclear Fuels Limited, the band Limp Bizkit came to town. Me and one of the men from work had been planning on going for a couple of weeks beforehand. I was living in a quasi-Bohemian community called Maplehurst Park at that time. It was adjacent to campus right down on the riverfront. This was one of the last affordable places to live downtown by the water because the yuppie condos and arrogant law firms had taken over most of the area by then. It was just a little ole slacker, hole in the wall, bachelor pad, but I loved it. As a matter of fact, I had lived in that very same building about four years earlier when I met my ex-wife. She had moved in with me for about a year while we were engaged and nagged me to move us to the Northwest side of town which I hated. As soon as we had separated after two years of marriage, I quickly migrated back downtown. Luckily, the place was under new management and the new manager and her secretary had no idea that I had flown by night just a few years earlier after I had fucked up a refrigerator trying to defrost it with a screwdriver and skipped out on my lease as well. Anyway, back in my old neighborhood, I was comfortable and within walking distance to most of my favorite party districts, including: The Cumberland Avenue Strip and The Old City as well as my Mecca, Neyland Stadium and The Thompson/Boling Arena (now known as The Summitt). I was still in the habit of heavy binge drinking even a decade after college and had just started experimenting with drugs. Having had a DUI in '91, I was still very careful about drinking and driving. Plus, I had just financed a hot new Firebird and didn't want to mess that thing up either. I figured if I was going to continue getting smashed, I would rather risk getting a PI, than another DUI (because I could keep my license that way) and luckily, I never got one, but had several close calls with the law though anyway, more of which I will get into later. The Stadium, however was only a fifteen minute walk away on a trail under the train trestle and I could crawl back to the crib blind drunk if I had to. And, the Arena was just west of there.

Anyway, back to that Friday night. They wanted us to work overtime on the following Saturday as they always did at a rate of about $18 an hour which was pretty good money at the time, but we were more interested in partying and chasing tail. I had recently arranged a fake driver's license for my friend who was 19 or 20 at the time so he could buy alcohol and get into bars, and to show his appreciation, he and another man had brought over some new pre-concert party favor that I had never tried before called crank. I did not know much about meth at the time except that it was some relatively new rural redneck concern made out of vile chemicals, but I figured I would give it a whirl since they had gone to the trouble of bringing it over. It was colored pink and looked a little like Draino. I had picked up a half a case of Michelob on the way back from work and had had a couple before the boys arrived and they had brought some beers too. I allowed the new guy to turn my toaster on its side and he chopped us out three lines. Luckily, there was a Mrs. Winners cup of iced tea in the fridge from the night before and I grabbed the straw and cut about a quarter of it off. Being a rookie with this stuff, I let the other two go first and then I leaned over and snorted up what was actually a pretty fat line compared to the way I had seen blow presented before. Within a minute, I could feel and taste that nasty shit running down my throat. After standing around staring at each other for a few minutes, I thought "is that all there is?" I asked them if I could do a little more and the guy apprehensively put out about a quarter of the original dose for me which I promptly did, but they did not take anymore. I really did not feel any buzz, but I passed out two beers apiece and locked the place up and we chugged them as we trekked over to The Arena.

Tickets for that show were pretty expensive as most concerts were at the time and since I was making pretty good money then, I could easily afford it; however I had something else in mind, a scheme. I left the other two guys at the upper East ramp to buy tickets from a scalper and told them I would catch up with them inside because I had a plan.

I was wearing a flannel shirt, jeans, and a $150 pair of steel toed boots with an electrical safety layer in the soles (every time I got a new union job, these companies would buy you a new pair of top quality boots and even if you got canned after a week, you got to keep 'em), but most importantly, I had some counterfeit Arena credentials which I had put together years earlier on one of my crummy data reproduction jobs. This unofficial Thompson/Boling Assembly Center & Arena STAFF badge upon rudimentary inspections, remarkably had allowed me access into many restricted areas of the facility over the years during major events; however, I had never actually used it to gain initial entry, but I had already tried something new that night so I thought "what the heck?". Anyway, I affixed the royal blue side of the I.D. to my shirt pocket which had a picture of me, the Arena logo, STAFF in bold face capital letters, the Name: B.H. Johnson, and Position: Electrical Engineer, and the security device (in the form of the University Crest halfway over the photo and half on the white part which I had drawn with a very fine point pen). I walked down the West ramp past the main entrances to the back where people came out to smoke. There were about twenty yards of steel barricades spanning across the ramp with a narrow portal in the middle guarded by a man and a woman in their late twenties. I popped in a piece of bubble gum to neutralize my beer breath as I mentally focused to get into character. "How ya'll doin?" I asked with a gruff Southern drawl. "Pretty good" they said "how bout you?" "Pretty good" I replied. "I'm the on-call Arena electrician" I said "and I was just relaxing at the house in the easy chair when they called me up and said to get over here because there's a problem with one of the transformers under the stage." They thought that was pretty bad. And, I asked "ya'll havin some kind of concert?---gravy biscuits or something?". "Yes Sir" they said "Limp Bizkit". "Hmm---Kids?" I said as I shook my head and they nodded. "Anyway, I hope I can just get it done and get out of here---would it be okay if I just go in here?" I asked. "Sure" they said "come on through" and they opened the gate. "Well, Thanks" I said "ya'll take it easy." "You too sir" they said as I cruised on in. Once I got past the smokers, I took off my badge and headed thru the back door. Once inside, I stopped by the bathroom on the mezzanine. After, I re-affixed my I.D., I went to one of the middle isles on the South side of the facility and nodded to the usher as I headed past his check point. He was wearing one of the canary yellow backed IDs for ushers only (which I had on the back of my blue one for technical staff.) Then I descended the stairs all the way down to the floor, pulling out the flathead screwdriver on my Gerber Tool where I met three guys in security shirts who obviously lifted a lot of weights; however, they did not look to be very bright. I held up my tool and told the fellows "my boss said there's some kind of problem with the number 13 wire up near the stage and I'm here to fix it." And, after considering this for a few seconds, one of them opened the blue velvet rope and allowed me to pass.

Now on the floor, I had to improvise a bit more because it was festival accommodations, which was extremely rare for that venue. I made my way thru the middle and then up to the right side of the stage. There was a dense crowd packed into an about 15x15 yard square area between me and center stage. Think, Think, Think; what could I do? Then I took off my badge and held it in the air with as much bogus authority in my right hand and in the other raised the screwdriver and announced "Alright people, there's a problem with the wiring at center stage, I need to get through here." They all looked crazily and unemotional towards me, obviously as high as I was, however I think I was holding it together a little bit better though. Then I loudly repeated " I need to get through here people!...You'll have no Limp Bizkit tonight unless I get up there!" And suddenly, the crowd parted quickly all the way to center stage and I headed forward. Once I got up there to the plywood barricade, I looked to the floor and there was a piece of duct tape sticking out from under it so I knelt down and mimicked like I was tinkering with something down there with the Gerber. Then I stood up, turned around and gave them the thumbs up and the devil's horns and shouted "Let's Rock!" and the crowd cheered wildly and closed back in around me.

In a little while, Method Man and Red Man came out (at least I believe they were the opening act that night.) I think those two were once in a consortium called The Wu Tang Clan with Old Dirty Bastard and then went on to Harvard to make a film "How High." Anyway, they put on a pretty good show and towards the end, they threw out a white cotton towel which I caught. This was fortuitous, because I was sweating almost as much as they were and used it to mop my brow. After a short break, Limp Bizkit came out and rocked! They were at, I believe the pinnacle of their popularity at the time, and not quite as irrelevant as when I would see them a few years later opening up for Metallica at Turner Field in Atlanta. After the show, which did have a lot of energy, the bouncers were bossing everyone to hurry up and get out of there, but on my way out, I spied a large pick on the floor (inscribed "Dumb Stupid Pick.") I picked It up with a few pieces of confetti (it was a very confetti rich environment) and when I got home, put them into the front of their current CD which I had won from the radio station. I always like getting a pick, even if it is a dumb and stupid one.

I stayed up all night that night and all day Saturday a little wired I guess and ended up at a house party off The Strip till about 3 a.m. Sunday morning. I told one of my friends from the Cross Country Team about the meth and how long I had been up and he asked me how I felt "Not bad" I said "a little tired." And he replied "Well, you look great!" However, I think he may have been a little euphemistic though, because---I felt like shit. Shortly afterwards, I hiked on home, took a few Ativans to chill out, slept all day Sunday and Sunday night, and went back to work on Monday.

Athens Road Trip I

It was shortly after Hurricane Andrew had devastated South Florida and the Vols were scheduled for a big showdown with the Dawgs. On Friday, I took a half a day off at the mailroom from International Harvester and cruised on down to Chattanooga in the Samurai to pick up my Big Brother and rendezvous with my former Pledge Educator who was on leave from the Air Force and the missile silos of South Dakota. We ended up taking Tony's Montero and made pretty good time to Atlanta and then over to Athens. One of our old Haneous Bitch buddies Moony, was attending graduate school at UGA in Forestry and had offered to let us crash that weekend. It was a slow night and we all sat around and reminisced only drinking a couple of Old Milwaukee's because we didn't want to hurt in the morning and planned to blow it out at the game (or at least that was my plan.) Our other brother Joe was supposed to meet us down there, but he had just graduated from pharmacy school on a government load and the man needed him to help out with Andrew relief in Florida. There was an incredible blue sky that day and the temperature was perfect. UGA had a beautiful campus and the co-eds were extremely hot to boot. The game was a sellout and tickets were hard to find but, somehow we managed to get three together in the corner of the end zone for not too much money. There was a quarterback controversy that year like so many other ones over the years which Coach Fulmer always tried to stage at the beginning of the season to encourage competition; instead of just getting behind one guy and sticking with him. That year it was between Heath Schuler (now a United States Congressman) and another guy, but Schuler really came on to lead them that day and I believe, he started the rest of the season after that.

I do not remember much of that game though past the first few series because we had sneaked in a fifth of George Dickel and I believe that I was hitting it a little bit harder than the rest of the guys (although my buddy from the military was not drinking that day) and on an empty stomach also. I do remember that we had excellent seats though. They were right in the front row of the balcony overlooking the end zone as well as the graves of their beloved mascots UGA and a nice monument to the dog. I remember that a nice older lady, a Georgia fan was sitting next to us and offered me some of her Cheetos which was her first mistake, because from then on I had bogarted the whole bag until I turned it up to get the last crumbs. What a pig I was that day, and a drunk and obnoxious one to boot. The only thing much that I remember after hogging all of the corn puffs was that after a big play for the Vols, I had jumped up to cheer and my buddies and that lady had to grab hold of my belt to keep me from falling over the balcony. I sobered up just a hair at the end of the match which we barely won but, they say it was a pretty good game. I had left the group for a few minutes to walk down to break off a piece of the hedges as a souvenir and then coming back out, I realized I needed to take a piss but I knew I was too drunk to find a restroom in time. So, I just whipped it out in front of UGA I's grave and started peeing. I was trying to read the markers on the wall and pee at the same time so I not only ended up peeing on UGA I's grave, but also on UGA II, II, and IV's graves as well. I then started walking to the right and then turned around and shook it on the statue. I guess I was in a little bit of a stupor because, when I looked up, there was a large contingency of Georgia fan shouting and cussing at me from the stands. Realizing my transgressions, I took off back under the end zone bleachers where I luckily met back up with the guys and some other fans we had knew from Knoxville.

After leaving the stadium; Tony, Mike, and I were walking through some slacker party neighborhood and somehow, I got separated from them in that they were a little ahead of me. Then somebody in the front yard of a house yelled "Hey you, come over here." And, like a drunken idiot, I did. Once I was in the yard, guys started coming out of the house. I am not sure how many there were, about fifteen or so, and they surrounded me. They started shoving me and saying, "you Tennessee Boys are pretty tough aren't you?" "Hey man, I'm a lover, not a fighter" I offered, but they were obviously poor sports after such a tough loss from us or perhaps, they may have witnessed my little post game tribute to their favorite mascot. Either way, there was still no way out but, I thought I should go down fighting and the last thing I could remember was taking a big swing at the lead redneck. Next thing I knew; Mike, my old Pledge Educator was picking me up off of the sidewalk. He said that when he came back; my head was lying in the bushes, my torso on the sidewalk, and my legs were out in the street, and that cars were just driving around me in the road. Tony had wound up at some house party down the street but, Mike had noticed me missing. He said that The Navy Seals didn't leave a man behind and he wasn't about to leave me either and he proceeded to escort and help limp me out of that rough area for about 6 or 7 blocks to the safety of a Waffle House where the waitresses kindly hooked me up with some ice for my battered face. I really appreciate my Delt Brother rescuing me that day as I have done for other brothers over the years. And I also appreciate the Women of Waffle House as well as a kind carload of cute sorority girls from campus who stopped to administer first aid. That night, I slept it off in the back of Tony's SUV and they checked on me every so often while they were running around to make sure that I was not dead from a concussion. We eventually got back to Moony's and slept late and then went out for breakfast. I felt like crap with a bad hangover on top of that beating on Sunday but, I still made it back to work on Monday albeit a little scuffed up. Suffice it to say, I was somewhat more well behaved and respectful the next time I went down for a football game, although I kind of managed to get a little shit faced (or rather completely stinking drunk and had blacked out for most of the day,) when LJ and I went down there for that big Widespread Panic show on the square but, that is another story.

9

The Angry Circus Midgets

It was a cold night in February or March. Tony, Holmes, and I were closing down The Last Lap and they were serving $1 Pabst Blue Ribbon tall boys. It was around 2 a.m., standing in the back, we started pounding beers with three burly looking guys who claimed to be roadies with The Ringling Brothers, Barnum, and Bailey Circus which had been in town for the last few days. And, they invited us back to their circus train to hang out and party with them after the bars closed. This sounded interesting so we told them we would meet them down there, whereas their trains were parked just down the hill behind our fraternity house at the train yards. Anyway, we picked up a couple of 12 packs of Natural Lite (it was "the beer with the taste for food" even if you didn't have any food ") at Gus' and headed down old fraternity row until we got to Volunteer and then we followed the train tracks South to avoid the University Police until we got to the circus encampment. There were about four rows of silver passenger cars with the Ringling Brother's logo on the sides. We entered the farthest train on the right from the North and it was somewhere between 3:45 or 4 a.m. Once inside, we knocked on the first compartment on the left, beer in hand and a sleepy but good looking brunette opened up and said "can I help you?" She appeared to be one of those Pseudo-foxy elephant riders who still had a little bit of glitter in the corner of her eye from the previous night's performance and was eating a plate of peas and carrots. We proudly announced that we were here to party! And, she replied "we're sleeping." " But we met these guys..."we said and she retreated. After she closed her door, this may have been a little ill advised, but we started running through the train shouting "Woo-hoo! ... where's the Fat Lady?, where's the bearded clam?" "We wanna party!" Once we got off the train, we were in between two rows of them about 15 yards apart. Scratching our heads and catching our breath; we were still buzzed quite a bit and on the verge of walking hangovers. It was foggy and when I looked up, we were surrounded by about fifteen of the most agitated and menacing looking circus midgets you had ever seen. They were all dudes and they spoke in the same manner as the ones in The Wizard of Oz, however they were not quite as friendly and the tone was much angrier. "What are you all doing here?" they shouted, but their voices were so silly and with us still buzzing, we could not help but break out in uncontrollable laughter. This unfortunately made them more menacing as they closed in. In between laughs I volunteered "some of ya'lls crew invited us down here to party." "Who invited you?" one of them demanded! "Some roadies, I guess...?" as I casually opened a beer which wasn't real cold anymore. "Bullshit!" They exclaimed "this is our home, you think this is funny??...This is where we live!" "How would you like it if we came over to your house and started raising hell?" one said. I uttered "I don't guess that would be to cool; we're sorry man...would you like a beer?" "Hell No!" they shouted in their squeaky yet gruff little voices as the moved in closer. I could not tell if they were armed with blackjacks, but instead, it looked like they were pulling out some of those little foot long bats that they give away to kids at a promotional night at a baseball game. I leaned back to my brothers and told them that they couldn't be very fast with such small legs and that we ought to make a run for it back to the house. We agreed on three and I picked up the remaining half case of Naties and in a V formation (like on kick-off returns), us ole

Haneous Bitches bolted on through their crowd. We made a bee-line between two of those train cars and over the coupling while at the same time getting beaned from those little bats that they were throwing at us. This connection slowed them down quite a bit and we scooted between two more sets of passenger cars the same way. And, from there, it was less than a five minute walk back to The Shelter. We were a little winded and covered with thick grease stains on our hands and across our clothes and I was pissed that I had ruined my favorite Polo shirt. Anyway, we jumped into the shower and then hit the sack because we all had early labs at 7:30 a.m. I guess the moral of the story here is " to let sleeping midgets lay."

The Lincoln Day Ordeal

Exiled from Oak Ridge for extreme manic behavior, my good friend and fraternity brother LJ had kindly taken me into his condo at Cherokee at Westcliff. My little red beater truck had been knocked out of commission a few weeks earlier and I was once again relegated to the status of a walker which I hated. Although things had gone terribly, terribly wrong for me since the meltdown, I had decided to try to keep up appearances and still maintain some kind of connection with the local Republican Party and I felt that the best way to do this would be to attend my county's yearly Lincoln Day Event. After all, I was still on the Vice-Chairman's Committee and a Precinct Chairman I assumed.

Anyway, it was cold and rainy that morning when I left the condo. It took me about 45 minutes to walk down that hill to the bus stop on Kingston Pike in front of the Krispy Kreme flagship store. It took a while for the bus heading west to get there and I was cold, only having worn a white button down Oxford shirt, Navy Brooks Brothers suit, dark blue tie, dark socks, and black wingtips. And, for some fucked up reason, I had been going to a black barber shop for a while, and had decided to get a real full mow hawk that was even shaved on the sides and was sporting a Fu-Manchu goatee at the time also. After transferring buses at West Town Mall, I talked to the driver and determined that she could only take me part of the way to my destination before she had to cross the interstate and that I would once again have to walk. The walk was only less than a mile, but it had started raining again and I felt gross. I was already about 35 minutes late and when I arrived at Rothchilds, I recognized a familiar face outside of a man who was re-attaching a sign for the event that the wind had blown down. I asked him "do I need to go ahead and buy a ticket (they were $25 or $30)?" And, he said "no, you can just go on in Buck." I said "thanks" and did. I went thru the buffet and loaded up with some pork chops and mashed potatoes and gravy, I think, and I respectfully chatted with a local law enforcement officer about the weather as I headed into the main ballroom. Coming through the doors, I could see the Hall Political Machine table was full with their usual crew including Stacey Campfield and I knew Tim was probably up front with one of his hot girlfriends so I discreetly headed to one of the far left tables in the back of the room where there was a couple and one other man. I do not remember who was speaking at the time but I think it was Dr. Bill Frist, The Speaker of the United State Senate. After a courtesy nod to the three around the table, I got a chance to look thru my goody bag of doo-dads and political paraphernalia and it was one of the lamest collections I had ever seen, but I got in free and was eating so- what the heck? I had just dug into my pork chops when a black man in a black suit tapped me on the shoulder. He had some kind of communications device in his ear when I turned around and said "What boy?....I'm eatin." "Sir, you need to come with me" he curtly replied so I picked up my plate and started to head out with him. " Sir, you need to leave your plate" he said.---Getting led out of the side of the banquet hall during a Lincoln Day speech...How embarrassing...Who could be behind this I wondered? I bet this was all that Bill Haslam's doings because I had criticized him on talk radio in favor of Councilman Hall for Mayor. That sorry fucker!

Once outside the hall, I was met by a wide array of law enforcement agencies, of at least a dozen men including: The United States Secret Service, Knoxville City Police, Knox County Sheriff's Department, The Tennessee State Highway Patrol, and I believe a special detail from the Governor's office. They turned me around and quickly had me up against the wall for a thorough search. "What seems to be the problem?" I asked, "Shut the fuck up, we'll ask the questions!" someone barked. After discovering about half a dozen assorted knives and box cutters, the man reached into my breast pocket and gleefully shouted "A-ha!" as he pulled out a baggy of pipe tobacco. "A-ha, what "I said? And once again they told me to "Shut the Fuck Up!" After they had found 6 or 7 more cutting instruments stashed at various parts on my person, they let me turn around and stand at ease. They asked "What was I doing there?" " Eatin" I said and that "I was a member of The Party." "Where's your ticket?" they said and I told them "that I got in free." Then a couple of Knox County Sheriff's Deputies recognized my Lodge belt buckle and stepped forward to exchange friendly grips and I thought that was a nice gesture but, I was still pissed at Haslam. Shortly, some other agents came over and told me that the manager of the facility had requested that I leave the premises." And, simultaneously some goober from Rothchild's handed me his business card! "Yeah right, you fucker, I'm going to have my next thousand dollar a plate fundraiser here after this shit!" I Snarled. "I get better food at the ball game" and laughed. I started to tear up his card and drop it at his feet but, the way things were going that day, I figured they would probably have me thrown in Federal Prison for littering of something. Meanwhile, another fellow campaign operative and friend of mine who would later go on to become a black caucus basher was being questioned and searched in a nearby room because he had rushed to my aid to vouch for me so the authorities figured he was a trouble maker or subversive too. I found out about this later and thought that was a nice gesture though on his part. Anyway, they handed me all of my shit back and I humped it East back up Kingston Pike re-stashing my stuff along the way until after a few blocks I arrived at Shoney's where luckily, they still had their breakfast bar out. They had some killer biscuits with sausage gravy (which was good-because some stores don't have meat in their gravy, but this one did!).

Unfortunately, like an elephant, I held a terrible grudge against our future Mayor for 8 or 9 months until the Senator finally let me know that it was Dr. Frist who turned the dogs on me that day at Rothchilds and not Mayor Haslam. Obviously, The Speaker of the United States Senate did not find any humor in my Taxi Driveresque hairdo and he profiled me as some sort of crazed urban terrorist who was stalking him...What a puss! I guess, looking back, I could have left a little more of that cutlery on the dresser that morning however, I was certainly no threat to any of my fellow Republicans. Hell, I had even voted for the man and kept his autographed picture my other favorites like Speaker Newt Gingrich and Lt. Col. Oliver North. I was a loyal foot soldier for the GOP was what U.S. Congressman Zach Wamp once told former U.S. Senator Howard Baker at a Republican event in Oak Ridge.

My relationship with The Mayor has improved a lot since then and now, he treats me just like one of the guys. As for Mr. Frist, I hope they run him out of the beltway on a rail (like in Oh Brother, Where Art Thou?) for his alleged insider trading and stem cell nonsense As the proud Chairman of The Anderson

County Young Republicans, I traveled to Atlanta, Georgia to convene with the rest of the Tennessee Delegation for our National Convention in the summer of '96. It was being hosted by one of those overpriced Peachtree...something or another hotels downtown. Having left the wife at home that weekend, I took the opportunity to drink to extreme excess and embarrass myself on several occasions during this period.

Young Republican National Convention

I guess the debauchery started the first night at the Tennessee Y R's hospitality booth, (sponsored by who else?...Jack Daniels of course.) I had burned out on bourbon pretty early in my drinking career and was more into Tanqueray Gin at the time; however, I felt compelled to show out with a barrage of JD shots. And, instead of drinking everyone else under the table, I ended up under our display table. I got some help getting up and the next thing I know, we were out on the sidewalk watching a nice parade. I think one of my buddies from the Chattanooga Club had shoved me out into the street, because suddenly, I was marching (or staggering) in the parade. Things were a little foggy in my head, but we seemed to be chanting in unison, "G-O-P,G-O-P,G-O-P!"...I shouted proudly, pumping my fist into the air. Right about then, someone tapped me on the shoulder and said "hey, it's great that you're coming out!" And after that, they draped a full-sized rainbow colored flag over my shoulders. "G-O-P, G-O-P,G...O...What?...the hell are you talking about?" I asked. "G-A-Y, G-A-Y, G-A-Y,!" they shouted with glee..."come on brother, join in," they implored. And then, suddenly it occurred to me that it was also Gay Pride Weekend in Atlanta and that I was actually marching in a G, L, B, and T Parade. As I seemed to have one of those moments of clarity that some alcoholics talk about, I immediately handed them their flag back and as discreetly as I could in my whiskey addled condition retreated back to the safety of the sidewalk. And, my friends were just guffawing and seemed to get a big kick out of the whole scene.

Anyway, later that night, I blacked out and got separated from our group and ended up passing out in the stairwell of the hotel. Some black goons in puke yellow colored blazers with the hotel logo woke me up and asked me "if I was a guest at the hotel?" "Yes, of course," I stammered, "What room are you in?" one of them asked. I didn't know because I was shit faced when we checked in and wasn't paying any attention...We had just dropped of our bags and headed for the nearest bar. Anyway, they handed me my wallet, which they said "was laying nearby me" and upon later inspection was about a hundred twenty dollars lighter than before. I don't remember spending that much on drinking that night, especially since the Jack was free. They then took me to a party at about 2 or 3 in the morning, where I recognized some folks and they let me go in. Before those men left, being totally stupefied, I thanked them for escorting me back to the others. And, I remember some girl from the Cheatham County Y R's laughing and making fun of me because, it was allegedly the hotel security guys, who had rolled me of my cash and that I was so stupid, I had thanked them for their help. Pretty mean spirited comments from a fellow Tennessean, I thought. I heard later, that she was a loose woman anyway. Later, that night, I had become so obnoxious, that the leaders of our delegation had to lock me into the hospitality lounge of our suite for my own good. I can remember crawling around on the floor and banging on the floor for them to let me out, but eventually, I passed out again.

I felt like shit the next morning, but had wanted to meet United States Senator Phil Gramm who was speaking at a luncheon downstairs that was halfway over. I was an early wagon puller for his campaign for President and was interested in getting a photo op with him. So I managed to get on a button down, tie, navy blazer, and khakis and made it in for the last few minute of his speech. And, on his way out of the dining room, I tossed my camera to one of his entourage and they actually snapped a nice picture of the Senator and I, which subsequently appeared in The Clinton Courier with the caption "Anderson County Young Republican Chairman Buck Cochran meets with Presidential candidate-Texas Senator Phil Gramm at YR National Convention in Atlanta." I'm just glad that the folks back home had no idea what a waste-toid I had been on that trip. What was so ironic was that one of my traveling buddies, who was almost as much of a drunk and pill-head as I was told me to "straighten up and, that these were all the national movers and shakers from all across the America that we would be dealing with for the rest of our lives and that he didn't want me to be remembered like this, all fucked up. I agreed and did straighten up for the balance of the trip, however coming from that guy it was like the pot calling the kettle black it seemed at the time.

I did get pretty down on myself though and called home to my wife with concerns that I may have an alcohol problem and felt embarrassed down there and wanted to come home early. The situation was though, that I did not drive all the way to Atlanta, only to Chattanooga and would just have to behave and tough it out. She was encouraging to me though and I think that we may have actually had some genuine moments of real love during my little three year marriage experiment, however they were few and far between, and even now, the veracity of those few minutes is debatable.

The Girl From Bambi's

Bambi's Last Chance Theater had always been my favorite strip club in Knoxville; I always thought they had the hottest dancers, but there was one in particular last I especially liked. I hadn't necessarily spent that much money on her initially with respect to personal dances, those $7 fruit drinks, $5 roses, or other club gimmicks, however I did max out a $1000 credit card over the period of a month to wine and dine her. It was the spring of '99 and I had made a promise to myself to cut back on my drinking and avoid getting fucked up in public because I wanted to run for City Council in the Fall. It took several attempts to get this woman to meet me outside of the club. And one night, after she got off, she told me to follow her in my Firebird. It was a long drive into Union County in the middle of the night and we ended up at an isolated and dilapidated trailer in the sticks. There was another man there when we arrived and she introduced him as her brother. Thing were really strange and I didn't get any that night. In fact, the inside of that mobile home was empty except for a couple of pieces of furniture and a dried up Christmas tree. And, the only thing in the bathroom was a tube of toothpaste. The whole joint had a very uneasy feeling about it. I really didn't feel like getting with her that night anyway after that creepy scene and weird visit, so I booked.

About a month later, she and that guy were living in a house in a ghetto over in South Knoxville. She had a rocket body, despite the fact that she had about five or six children. I took her to expensive restaurants, trendy clubs, and concerts for a month. She did not have a phone, so whenever I wanted to see her, I had to chance it and drive across the river.

One day, at a UT Basketball game, I won a very nice cellular phone in a trivia contest and without having noticing it was gone, the girl had bogarted it. Her barrowing it in itself would not have been so bad except, when the battery ran down, for some fucked up reason, she cut the cord off of a lamp and attached the live wires to the phone and it exploded. Her brother raised hell with us about ruining his lamp, because he thought that we were using the cord for bondage.

As it turned out, the woman was a morphine addict, however since I was always fucked up on benzo's, I let her drive the Bird quite a bit and she really like driving that car. Sometimes, we would end up way out in the country at a trailer or shanty and I would have to wait out in the car for her. I later found out that she was servicing those residents for hands full of pills. She was very adept, so I could see where it was probably a pretty good deal for those ole boys though.

Finally, at one point in my life, I had put together the 4 quarter keys to what I had imagined would be a complete and happy life: a good job, a cool pad, a fast car, and a hot girlfriend. The House of Buck was finally in order!

Then, about halfway through this world wind romance, her "brother" told me that she had multiple personalities; about 17 or so (and, I just thought she was crazy as fuck!) and for some reason she was very jealous of my estranged wife. I remember, one time at my place, we were in bed together right after she had just taken her tongue ring out, and my ex-wife called. She encouraged me to tell the wife that I was with her now and that she should beat it. One thing that which was interesting was that after the first time we had just had sex, she asked me to buy her an early pregnancy test at Walgreen's and she took it right there in the front seat! "Yep I'm pregnant" she said "and it's yours." And, I said " I didn't know that those things could indicate conception or gestation in an hour?" But, she did not know what I meant. Incidentally, shortly after I learned of her illness, I was on top of her making out over at the ghetto retreat and I looked up and the four year old boy is sneaking up on me with a baseball bat! When I asked him what he was up to, he told me that his momma's sugar daddy promised him a hundred dollar bill if he would bash my brains in! Needless to say, intimacy was a little strained at the residence after that.

Then, about a week later, I came over and had just missed her according to her "brother." Anyway, that guy asked me "if I liked coffee?" Hell yeah I did; strong and black! Back in the kitchen, we started drinking on a pot of JFG, and as it turned out, he informed me that he was really her husband! Wow...So not only did she have a sugar daddy and a faux boyfriend, she was also married! The coffee was good though and the conversation was friendly. "So why this whole game?" I asked "I'm not rich?" "Well, she really likes that car of yours and was thinking that you might give it to her" he explained. "Oh, is that all? Yeah, I can see me paying almost $400 a month just to give a car away which I don't even own" I said. "I could just walk to Oak Ridge for work every day!" "Anyway, why are you just telling me this now?" I asked. And he replied "well, you just seem like a nice guy and I hate to see you taken advantage of this way." "It had gone on long enough" he said. I really appreciated his candor and good taste in coffee so I split and didn't go around there again.

I did see her back at that club a few months later and she told me that her "brother" had moved out of state and that everything he told me was lies, but I just blew her off and left.

I have only been back to that club one other time since then. I think I paid a $10 cover one night and I gave the barmaid another ten for a $2 bottle of water. Then she only gave me change for a five. When I asked for the rest of my change, she turned into a rude bitch. Then, when I asked to speak to the manager, some fatheaded monster, who looked like he was on steroids comes out in a ridiculous looking cheesy tuxedo and asks me "if there's a problem?" "Of course there's a problem" I said " I gave her a ten for a bottle of water and she gave me change for a five. She said "you're wrong" he said. "Well, I've been coming here for years and never had a problem like this" I said. And then, the meathead suggested "if I was so unhappy I should just leave." "Not without that cover, I want it back!" I protested.

"Well, you're not getting it back!" he exclaimed. What a fuck head, I thought. He had absolutely no concept that the customer is always right. Anyway, I never returned, and don't recommend that club to anyone.

Supporting The Team

I guess I had been making counterfeit passes and credentials to University of Tennessee football games at Neyland Stadium since the early nineties. It was the waning day of a happy era with Presidents Reagan and Bush and the start of something very sinister and dark known as the Clinton Administration. I remember well after Slick Willie's election that November, that it seemed to have rained or been overcast for nearly three weeks in K-town.

I was working as a Lead Mailroom Clerk (Woo-hoo, look at me, the college boy, a real leader!) for some bullshit outfit called Cobble Personnel. She was a real corporate hot-shot who even had her own employment advice column at the top of the garbage of want ads on Sunday in The Sentinel. Looking back, I reckon she was to business and fucking workers over to what Councilwoman xxxxxxx xxxxx was to political arrogance in Knoxville. Ms. Cobble was so much larger than life and esteemed among Knoxville business leaders that they even named her Chairperson of The United Way's corporate pan-handling drive one year. She wasn't paying us shit, and the benefits sucked, yet she would drag us into these Manchurian Candidate-style sessions to make us watch videos exploiting poor crippled children and told us that she expected 100% participation from our facility. After the marathon of propaganda, she had a brief question and answer forum. After a bunch of garble from the big givers and suck-asses in Marketing; I could not help but throw in a small query for my homeboys in the Mailroom. I stood up " Ms Cobble- Buck Cochran...Data Reproduction and Mailroom Coordinator" "Yes Buck?" She replied. "Could you comment on the recent allegations of the United Way CEO and other top officer's opulent embracement of the High Life including first class limousine transportation as well as frequent trips on The Concorde?" "And, how can we be assured that our contributions will go to help worthy local agencies like the Boy's and Girl's Clubs and not to support the arrogant lifestyles of a bunch of highbrow fat-cats in New York City?" She was kind of speechless after that and giving was subsequently down at our facility, but hell; inquiring minds wanted to know! And besides, Dealer Services said that there was twenty bucks in it for me if I axed? I was on the company shit-list for years anyway because of my lack of support for their trendy and stupid Demming-Japanese style of "team management" and the fact that we were all going to be under the cheesy Lee Press-On thumb nail of the Donna Cobble Company for peanuts without ever getting a chance to work directly for the big boys at International Harvester. I did hear about a decade later that a few of them had made it with the real company of Navistar which was good for them, I guess. I did however have a few good memories of there and personally I liked a lot of the workers at the facility with the exception of Ms Cobble's goose-stepping onsite, human resource managers (the last of whom planted a Never Hire Again!...memo in my personnel file) but, I did have a cool old boss name Gene who put up with a lot of my hateful and angst ridden bullshit for nearly three years. He knew how bad I hated it there, but I really tied to be nice eventually and he wrote me some pretty nice performance reviews that he didn't have to and I appreciated that. And, the ladies in the data key crew were always nice to me and sometimes, I would even give them neck massages so that they wouldn't get so tense from all that typing.

Anyways, enough with the niceties...most folks who really knew me knew, that the only reason I held on to that crappy job for nearly 35 months was so that I could hone my skills and operate my own clandestine print shop on the side -The Cochran Press. As for the copier, I think that the name of that old behemoth was the Xerox 9900 (which I had been formally trained on at The Boeing Company...another sorry outfit) and one of my old fraternity brother's wife's father was my repairman. I had had a crush on his other daughter at one time and I do not think that he liked my drunkard ass. I think that the low rent fuckers at Navistar had probably purchased this ragged out monster after it was almost completely depreciated and possibly earmarked for a third world country. When it wasn't down though, I still managed to push a quarter million copies of that business bullshit thru it every month. Then, I finally got to work on my own projects like making fake passes for individual University of Tennessee home football games including: sideline, concessions, press areas, and the corporate sky boxes. These little capers were purely for the amusement of myself and my old college buddies and in the nearly two dozen times we had infiltrated the various areas for different stunts affordable tickets were readily available.

Anyway, of all those years, a few incidents seemed to stick out in my bourbon soaked memory the most. One of these was a nice afternoon game against Alabama. Ahh. The 3rd Saturday of October. A clear blue sky, a cool breeze and about a dozen of my closest friends...it was a special time to be a Vol. This was pre-9/11 mind you and things were a little more laid back at the stadium then. We still had a tight knit group of hell raisin alumni (known as the FOG or Fucking Old Guys) who came in for nearly every game, especially the big ones. Almost all of the crew already had tickets and I managed to get one for twenty bucks, but that still left us one short. We all used to squeeze into those portable little bleachers up front so we could check out the cheerleaders better. I took a chance and told one of my buddies to give me twenty for my ticket and told him, I would meet them inside. I really did not want to miss the game (it was Bama...for God's sake!) but for the continuity of the brotherhood, I would sacrifice in the hope that we could all be there together. They all entered at the North Ramp and I headed around to one of those really old and decrepit gates on the lower East Side of the stadium. There were two good ole boy ticket takers and no police like there are now. The one on the left looked a little more corrupt than the one on the right and so I carefully folded that twenty into the size of a ticket and placed it in the palm of my hand as I casually headed towards the left side of the gate, palm raised where only he could see it, while at the same time, I maintained constant eye contact. Then he smiled and nodded after which I smiled also and waited a minute for someone else to come through on the right to distract the other man in case he was a preacher who might have an ethical problem with our left path arrangement (this was just precautionary and more than likely he wasn't that religious and they probably split their bribes 50/50.) Anyway, I handed it to him like a regular ticket which went right into his pocket and I went right thru the gate and up the tunnel. Once inside I rendezvoused with my party and we had pretty good seats like usual around the 35 or 40 yard line a few rows up on the Southeast side near The Pride of The Southland Band.

I was wearing Khaki Duck Heads, a dark Polo shirt, Campsides, no socks, gold Ray Ban Aviators (small lenses), and a Levis jacket with two half pints of Jim Beam stashed in my inside pockets. I chugged about half my Coke in the stadium cup and then filled it nearly full of bourbon. I guess I was not getting drunk fast enough and was a little bored so I covered my drink and headed down to the field, leaned over and told the sideline gate keeper "Knoxville News Sentinel" and he kindly opened the gate for me. These were the real good ole days when you could just bullshit your way down there with a good line and hardly ever needed a pass. Once down on the field you really hear the crowd roar, it was nearly as intoxicating as the liquor...well not really, but it was plenty loud and I went down to hang out near the UT cheerleaders for a while. I had just taken a big ole belt having forgotten that I had not stirred my drink and right then, the play came rushing past me so fast but for just a brief second, the TV camera was panning by me and I made the biggest scowl from that straight belt. Like I said...it was only for a split second, but my mentor and a bunch of other friends who were watching at home said "There's Buck!"they told me the next day.

Next, I moved over to check out the Bama cheerleaders, and suddenly this big black stud running back for the Tide came crashing down right in front of us and fumbled the ball out of bounds. I quickly sat my whiskey drink down and as the hot little Alabama cheerleader picked up the football, I leaned over, hands extended, like I was the ball-boy and she just tossed it to me. I quickly smiled and said "thanks whore" and walked away. Naturally I had to ham it up a little for the guys in the stands so I struck a Heisman pose at first and then like I was throwing a bomb and we laughed, them up there and me on the field still. It was getting near half time so I strolled down to the North end zone and headed out and some dude at the gate said "and where do you think you're going with that ball mister?" I quickly snapped that "I'm a blue-chip phenom punter from West Tennessee and I'm here on an official visit...the coach gave me this ball and if you piss me off, I'm going to commit to Florida you rube!" "Oh, I'm sorry son, go right ahead...sorry I didn't know." So anyway, I bogarted Jay Barker's game ball (with beat the cocks written on the laces) and walked out with my drink to boot. It was just an all around fun day!

Then, there was another year that I remember where Congressman Heath Shuler was up for the Heisman that season. We were not playing anyone too important, so I set my big brother up as a writer from Sports Illustrated and myself from the Associated Press. We were casually meandering down around the South tunnel (pretending to take notes) in the end zone and had struck up a conversation with a foxy red-headed news babe named Kristen Hoke. She was doing the weekend anchor for Channel 10 at the time and had a really nice caboose. We were just a couple of fellow journalists shooting the breeze about the news, you know, and me describing my illustrious career with the AP. Then, before I knew it, Tony was over there on the UT bench interviewing Shuler! Tony said that Heath said he was a big fan of SI and was glad to talk to him, but this was way beyond the protocol that I had set for this mission and he ended up getting busted by some real life university press liaison from the Sport Information Office. "Where'd you get this pass...?" he demanded of my friend. And, Tony just said he "bought it from some guy up in the North end zone." They then escorted him off of the field and as much as I liked chatting with Miss Hoke, I thought I had better get the hell out of there too. We would have to be more careful.

We did however have a big home game against Georgia the following Saturday and during that week some of my contacts in Nashville had informed me that in the paper over there, they had run an article stating that individuals had infiltrated the UT sidelines over the weekend with bogus credentials and that University Officials were going to be on the lookout at the Georgia game to catch them. There was not a word of this in any of the Knoxville Media outlets, whereas they did not want to tip us off. But I was brash, and wanted to try it just one last time. So, I affixed a bumper sticker pass to my ankle claiming I was with the Atlanta Journal Constitution. I went it alone that night and the pass looked pretty good, however less than ten minutes into the game back at my post near the South tunnel, some guy in a UT sport shirt came up to me and said "beat it!" And, I swiftly did back up into the student section. I guess the extremely loud Lindsey Nelson style plaid jacket I had worn that night was not a good choice...especially later. I do not remember much about much about the rest of that game until the end for I must have blacked out from those 2 pints of Jim Beam (not genuine without his signature) I had brought that night. Anyway, coming out of my stupor about half way through the fourth quarter, I found myself standing in front of the big donor section on about the 20 yard line of the Southwest side of the stadium down near where the Vol dancers are now. For some fucked up drunken reasoning, I got the great idea to sneak back onto the field (yeah, nobody would notice me in that loud jacket stumbling all over the place...). I managed to reattach my tattered and bogus credentials and went out onto the field, but the only problem I had was when I staggered out into the Southwest corner of the end zone; the game was still going on. Then things heated up a little when that goober from before shouted at me "Hey, didn't I tell you to get out of here earlier?" "No, it must've been somebody else" I muttered. Then I took a running leap for the south end zone wall (as the players sometimes do after a touchdown to celebrate with the fans.) I was frantically trying to pull myself up into the stands to escape but, the wall was tall and there were about 15 to 20 ushers and law enforcement officers from several different agencies grabbing my belt, pants, and shoes trying to pull me back down; not to mention the uncooperative fans on the first 2 rows who kept hitting me with their pom-poms and pushing me back. I am sure it was quite a spectacle and I am glad that no one had captured the melee on videotape? Anyhow, what happened next was a small miracle. Once down on the turf, they put my arms behind me. " You're in BIG TROUBLE BOY!" was all I could hear several times as they were hauling me off the field, so I shouted " Please, Please!...Let me go...my father is a huge contributer to this university!" I reckon the drunk tank must have been full that night or some Big Orange God was smiling down on me because when we hit the gate from the field to the stands; they let go of me. And, I took off running up thru the 50 year season ticket holder section (like an Under Armor commercial) and up and out of the stadium and I didn't look back till I got to The Torchbearer at Circle Park...Wheww!! Things were getting a little too hot on the field for those type of capers that I was running so I decided to take the rest of the season off until things cooled down a little. However, I did do a little advanced scouting for next season.

I had never been a guest in the new west side skyboxes and was a little curious to see exactly how those fat-cat contributors were living up there. So, I closely watched people getting on and off the inside elevator on the public floor near the top and studied the way things went. Then after a game, I was hanging out around the elevators on Stadium Drive and asked one of the catering service girls to give me her old work access badge for that day on her way out. After she left, I picked up a matching color, but different numbered tear of stub for that pass in a box of regular ticket tear off stubs for that day. After I taped these two together, I had a near perfect template for several seasons to come because the University never changed the style for years and years, using the same printing company and font even to I believe to this present day.

The next season came and I managed to get a connection on the catering staff who worked on the main luncheon they offered every week at half time. I would tweak the template all week at work and on Fridays before home games, during lunch I would stop at the If Its Paper store to pick some various hues of cardstock for the color of the week for all passes, while at the same time, she was picking up her real pass from her boss. Then, I would meet her at the Copper Cellar on Cumberland Avenue for $1 Long Island Teas. I would buy her a couple while I compared the pass to my cardstocks and usually got a perfect match. She had a kid and had to bounce after a drink or two, but by that time, most of the rest of the crew had arrived at our usual large table under the painting of the plump naked lady in the corner. Next, I would slide out and run over to Kinko's next door to print the passes. Even though I was pretty much a data repro pro by this time, you had to be careful with their equipment and load your own cardstock in their machines when the clerks weren't looking. I would usually run a proof or two on plain paper to get the density just right and then would run 5 copies thru with the cardstock fourth, because if you run it individually, sometimes the cardstock gets jammed or doesn't fuse right and sometimes an alarm goes off. And, I certainly didn't want a commotion with those copy geeks getting in my business after what happen to Jack Sells (although he was a true traitor to our program) at that store. I always carried a couple of extra sheets of stock, so if there was a jam, I could usually fix it pretty quick and reset the machine before anyone noticed. Uggh, enough with this technical bull shit! So I got one good sheet with four passes on it, double checked the glass, and got the hell outta there. Next, I went behind the building and destroyed all the extras and proofs that I had on me and threw them in the dumpster. Once back at the Copper Cellar, the rest of the guys were two or three teas ahead of me, so I raced a couple of them down in a hurry with those who were still nursing theirs. We also kept track of how many we had drank by the number of straws in your glass (this was one of the few occasions where it was okay for men to use straws.) By the time you had accumulated 14, or 15, or 16 in your glass, you could pretty much just put them all in your mouth and inhale it in a second. But dollar Long Island Tea nights at the Cellar were a completely different set of sordid stories in themselves. This was just a starting point though, before we all staggered and chunked our way East down the Strip to hit our other favorite bars.

Back to the passes, I usually felt a little rough on game day Saturday mornings, so I went over to the Varsity for breakfast and coffee until I felt a little better. Then when the shakes subsided, I managed to cut out the worker passes, perforate them with a technical knife, and tie some stretchy string around them so you could attach them to your belt loop (the lower down you could wear them, the harder to inspect.)

So the new goal for Tony and I was to infiltrate the executive skybox and dine with them, but this was a more complicated scheme. We got on the elevator when it was empty except for the good ole boy rent a cop and told him what floor we were going to (the one with all the food.) He said that he never got to see the games because he was working (poor fucker, I thought) and we told him we were executives with J P Sports. I took his address and told him I would send him a copy of the game that week, but we weren't able to due to video copyright restrictions. Once at the luncheon, I nodded at my girl as Tony and I took off our passes to blend in with the crowd. It was all the greasy potato chips and plain stadium vendor hot dogs you could eat...Yee-haw! Somehow, I expected cordon bleu or something more for what we were paying damn it! However, they did have a really kick-ass build your own sundae bar with some really luscious syrups and an equally luscious woman to top you off with real whipped cream, nuts and a cherry. After that we got bored. I told my friend " not to work too hard" and we boarded the elevator and went back down with the common folk...I mean real fans! Next week up there was different though.

The next week, I forget who we were playing (South Carolina or perhaps Arkansas), but I took my other fraternity brother LJ up there too. And, the elevator operator asked about the video from the week before. "No problem my good man" I said "we'll try again this week!" "Thank you Sir!" he said and smiled. Once we got up there, LJ's parents were in someone's corporate box and we stopped in for a visit. His dad knew what we were up to, looked at our passes, and just shook his head. Out in the lobby, it was crumby old hot dogs and chips again and not even any chili or Dijon mustard! What kind of low-rent production was UT Food Services trying to pull off here? The sundaes were awesome as usual and in some freezers, they even had some Fudgesicles and Brown Cows with cool little UT Vol wrappers to which we helped ourselves to a few. I had to take a leak so I walked down to the restroom at the North end of the skybox.. It was like Xanadu compared to the facilities in the rest of the stadium. I had no idea. After I had washed up and was coming down the hall, I found myself walking next to Athletic Director Doug Dickey. I don't know what came over me (maybe that pint of Captain Morgan's?), but I just put my arm around his shoulder and said "Coach?" "Yeah son?" he said. And then, with all the seriousness in the world I said "I don't care what they say about you, you're alright!" "Well, thanks and who the hell are you?" he queried. "A fan coach, just a fan" I replied and walked on ahead, grabbing a couple more UT Brown Cows out of the freezer where I met LJ and then we hopped on the elevator to rejoin the rest of the 100,000 plus

The Plant Days

After returning home to Tennessee from my exiled, drug crazed, pseudo-witness relocation work trip in Defiance, Ohio, I trained all Summer with the Laborer's Union so I could someday eventually go on to work at the same facility, in my hometown, which my father and grandfather had worked at. I already had the 40 hour HAZWOPER certification from before, and went on to learn about working safely in a nuclear environment as well as becoming certified in asbestos abatement also.

My first assignment at K-25 (also known as The East Tennessee Technology Park) was on a decontamination and demolition job at buildings K-724 and K-755, where I participated in asbestos and beryllium abatement in radiological areas as a laborer for Local 818, in November of 1997. This was a fairly easy job, as were most of my union gigs, whereas me, another man and two women worked on a support crew which mostly just backed up the main asbestos contractor. Most of the time, one of the women got to be the foreman and the other the steward and the other fellow and I just sat around the break room drinking coffee on most days. Occasionally, he and I would have to do some manual labor, but it was not too bad. Sometimes, the boss lady would have us dress out to go into the hot zone and help the other crew move some bags of asbestos or to do other chores but, it usually wasn't too hectic and most of the time I was able to eat some pills and smoke my tobacco pipe quite a bit. One time, they tried to get me and the other guy to decon the respirators for the whole crew at the end of the day, but we got out of that by putting up an official looking sign instructing the other men to wash their own and eventually, they started doing it every day! We did have to do shit some days, but by in large, it was a pretty leisurely job until I almost lost my finger.

This was the job where I first met my friend from the Iron Workers, as he was working as a Laborer on that site also, except that he was working for the main contractor. He was stressed out some like I was, however his doctor put him on Kolonopin, whereas mine had me on Ativan. I remember one time when we mixed and matched pills (kind of like those Reese's commercials); that was a pretty loopy day, especially considering, that I had just got my Bobcat license the day before, and was about to operate one of those things for the first time on that site. I was such a terror on that thing and was like a one man wrecking crew ripping the rafters down out of that building until I accidentally severed some hydraulic line going to the bucket (they don't make'em the way they used to!) I didn't read until later that the combination of those pills was potentially fatal.

I remember one day, the forewoman had me using some mixed-gasoline powered saw to cut some metal pipes. Unfortunately, the thing was dripping fuel on me and when the sparks started to fly, my fly caught on fire! I think I was wearing a hardhat and respirator and did not notice when the entire crotch and midsection of my Tyvek suit ignited as my Fire Watch did just that; and watched from a distance.

Fortunately, I did not panic, and was able to safely put the saw aside and then stamped out the fire with my gloved hands. And luckily, my boys didn't even get burned, because I was wearing heavy Carharts underneath!

Some days, out there, we would have to pick up cigarette butts behind the break room when the big bosses came in from the home office, so we could look busy. Some laborers found that chore to be demeaning. I did not smoke cigarettes at the time, but found it to be easy money and relatively safe compared to handling asbestos and being exposed to a big plume of beryllium dust we accidentally stirred up one day.

Everyone got along really well at that site and on a lot of days, we would all go out for drinks at the Sagebrush Steak House after work. One time the project manager, secretary, some other workers, and I went to see Matchbox 20 at the Civic Auditorium when they first came out. I got really fucked up on beer and pills for that show, and I'm glad that somebody else drove that night.

A lot of times, we worked four 10's, and one Friday that I was scheduled off, the boss lady called that day and asked me to come in. I told her I had a bad migraine that day, but she talked me into it anyway. This was before I had discovered Imitrex Spray, so I usually took a lot of Advil and a few extra chill pills to treat one. That afternoon, another laborer and I were standing in the back of a Baker-box on top of some bags of asbestos, and the site manager was bringing buckets of bags over in the Bobcat for us to unload. We were about 70 bags into it as I was standing there shooting the shit with my friend while I casually held on to the side of the container with my left hand to keep my balance. At that point, I unfortunately did not notice the boss driving the Bobcat up against the container until my fingers were smashed between it and the bucket! "Oh God!," I yelled. I jerked my hand back and ripped off my glove expecting to find bloody stumps. The pain was so bad; I had not cried like that since they cancelled "The Dukes of Hazard." They took me to the occupational health doctor for x-rays and a drug test to see if I was on any illegal substances, but I was not. I think one of my digits was broken and a couple of others were smashed pretty bad. My head was throbbing almost as bad as my hand and they turned the lights off in the examining room until the big boss got there. He ran into the room and lifted up my hand to make sure it was still there and to make sure that I was not going to sue them. This little accident shut the site down for a day or two during the investigation and I think that that guy may have lost his Bobcat license. I am just glad it was the curved side of the bucket and not the sharp side or I surely would have lost all my fingers that day. This job was wrapped up in March without any further incidents and I was fortunately able to collect unemployment as well as successfully apply to a state sponsored health insurance plan called TennCare.

I guess my ex-wife decided that we should split up about a week after she had graduated from college that spring and during that period the union got me on with the asbestos contractor for The University of Tennessee. This was the same company in charge of the abatement from my last job; however the superintendent on this campus-wide site was a hateful jackass. He believed in all kinds of shortcuts and thought that all those government regs, procedures, and protocols pertaining to the safe removal of asbestos were just a waste of time and only window dressing for the benefit of the ignorant students and staff over there. I hated that fucker...what a dickhead. I remember this one project in a manhole across the street from The Panhellenic and Strong Hall. The steam system was supposed to have been shut down for a day or so...some arbitrary number of hours to cool down before you could access it. These two drunken brothers, the superintendent used during the midnight shift, left some loose asbestos in the tunnel under the street, so that morning, he ordered me and another friend to go down and retrieve it. There were a lot of students walking by as it was between classes. The system was on full blast, and it was hot as a motherfucker down in that confined space. We both tried to go down there a couple of times individually while the other watched down in the hole, but the asbestos was about 15 yards away down a side tunnel under the street. It was so hot that we both nearly lost consciousness when we tried to go down that tunnel. The other laborer and I agreed that with just the two of us on this particular site, neither one of us would be able to rescue the other safely if one of us passed out. We did not have a belt retrieval system and if one of us had to attempt a rescue, there would be no one left to watch if the rescuer passed out too. I had seen one too many shortcuts over the last month, so I went to a pay phone to call another friend who was the Health and Safety Officer on my last job, to ask his advice. I told him my concern, that I didn't want us to fry our brains in a few minutes in that hole on a bullshit job like this, when we could live and go on to work 20 years at the plant in Oak Ridge. We all three agreed that I should shut down the job, which was a pretty serious maneuver, but I was convinced that this was an imminent danger to life and health situation...so we shut it down. The Client (UT) was pissed and within an hour, the Superintendent, Bubba, arrived at the site and told us that we were both furloughed. Being the vindictive fucker that I am, I contacted the local TOSHA office to tell them what happened and some investigator named Kirk took my written complaint. He said "This sounded serious, and that they would look into it." The next day, I watched from the parlor at Strong Hall as a couple of agents came over to the site to investigate. The manhole cover was back over the hole and all they did was stand around and chat with Bubba for a few minutes. What a joke! Kirk later told me that "we checked out your complaint and didn't find any problem at all." I had heard that Bubba had sent those two drunks down there that night after the incident to tidy up and close up the manhole. In my arrogant redneck opinion, TOSHA was just as corrupt and toothless as the EPA and TDEC were on that job that I had got run off from in Alcoa after cooperating with the FBI. I speculate that, TOSHA's Mr. Kirk just gave ole Bubba a courtesy call about that complaint and let him know that they would be coming for a visit the next day; the old boy network, I guess. And then, some folks had told me, that dirty fucker Bubba, had the audacity to make some calls to people over at K-25 to tell them not to hire me because I was a whistle blower. If he was so tough, that redneck fuck should have gone down in that hole himself to have had a heatstroke and die that day!

Then around Independence Day, I finally got the call I had been waiting for...the secretary from 818 asked me if I would like to go to work for BNFL or British Nuclear Fuels Limited. I was elated; this job had the potential to go on for years with some good pay. My ex-wife was there that day and I can remember her saying "this is great, now we can go on vacations!" And, I said "what do you mean we?...you're leaving." I had no idea at that point that I would fuck this one up, the way I had every other decent job I had ever gotten.

The first day I walked through the gate, I was heartily welcomed by my other union brothers from the last D and D job. I did not have a clearance and had to be escorted around the plant. Interestingly, my escort turned out to be Joe, a retired painter for whose yard I had mowed for the last 20 years that was assigned to me...how cool!

I had quite a few different jobs during my 16 months at that site as well as a few controversial incidents which occurred during that period too.

My first job was assisting sheet metal workers cut and disassemble an elaborate system of duct work. We worked for a while and played Rook for a while (I never could understand that game too well) rotating in and out of the containment area all day long because it was so hot, but not like that sewer at UT hot, just pretty warm. Sometimes, we used cool vests loaded with ice packs which I liked a lot, even though they got pretty funky at times. But we were wearing respirators most of the time and couldn't smell them too much anyway.

My second job would be scrubbing and degreasing huge transformer like units for a month or so. This was boring as fuck but at least we got to sit around on our asses all day, so I got to know my buddy from The Rock Concert Story pretty well and we ended up playing on the BNFL softball team together.

After that, I got on a crew where we had to scrape PCB gaskets off of some huge heavy metal pieces of duct work. I was always worried about getting my hands cut off if someone dropped one while I was working under it. During this time, I was partnered with a tall former college basketball player who was always irritating me. One day when we were coming out of the contamination reduction zone, we got into it, He shoved me and I told him to " back off bitch!" He responded by swinging at me and knocking my hard hat off. In a split second, I restrained, because I knew if I took a swing, I would more than likely get canned too. Another laborer next to us claimed that "he didn't see anything." Some kind of good ole boy code of silence I guess? Anyway, the tall guy got fired and I got a couple of days off without pay.

My next assignment was pretty tough and the next couple of months were very physically demanding and noisy. We were in a large containment tent wearing 2 pairs of flame retardant coveralls and respirators using saw-zaws to cut up those heavy metal pieces from before. One benefit of this assignment was that my forearms got pretty big like Popeye's, I guess?

During this period of my life, now that I was separated, I started to explore the world of exotic dance clubs a little more (not that being married ever kept me out of them too much to start with though.) *See Girl from Bambi's story.

More Plant Days

Later in the spring of '99, I got transferred to the Waste Management Operations Team. Then, we basically rode around in a golf carts in lab coats with clip boards checking for leaky drums. We kept records for compliance with RCRA, TOSCA, and CERCLA. This was real easy money, except the only thing that sucked was that I had to ride around and be escorted by a man named Billy Ray. He hated my ass because I had a reputation for being a staunch Republican, Being in the GOP was really incongruent with the union way of life because the Democrat Party had historically pandered to unions. Anyway, he harassed me every day, but he eventually laid off and was an important witness for me in a later incident. And, I think eventually went on to become the President of that Local 818.

The next incident at K-33 occurred one day when the Waste Management Operations Supervisor asked me and two other Laborers to use tow-motors to load a bunch of drums on the top floor into the freight elevator. Anyway, the Operator's got their panties all in a wad because we were taking their work and they complained to the health physics technicians. Plus, we overloaded the fuck out of that elevator and tore it up pretty bad. So then, the three of us Laborers ended up getting suspended without pay for three days just for following orders. 818 organized a big rally after that out on the main road, going into the plant to protest for us three...What great Solidarity! After that, they brought in some big wig, heavy hitters from the Laborer's International and they negotiated for us to get two days pay back, as a compromise so the company could save face. I was also in the process of joining the Free Masons at this time and garnered a lot of support and encouragement from the other brothers on the site.

If that was not enough conflict, soon after that, Billy Ray and I were going into the office and that same supervisor who fucked us over with that elevator deal, wrenched my arm in anger. This was a perfect opportunity to fuck him back, so Billy Ray and I immediately ratted him out to the company. Plus, being the media-hound I was, I made a quick call to the ORPD as well as several electronic news outlets. He got canned after about a week and also, my buddy from the Iron Worker's threatened to whip my foreman if he didn't get off my ass, to boot.

This seemed to be a strange time in my life, shortly before my diagnosis with Bi-Polar Disorder. It was spring and I had begun that bizarre relationship with the hot stripper for a while and I had unofficially decided that I wanted to run for Knoxville City Council that fall. At the same time, I was being investigated for a government clearance at the time and had foolishly admitted on the application that I had experimented with pot in college. That was extremely poor judgment on my part to mention that, thus fucking everything up and ultimately ending my career at K-25. So remember kids, always fucking lie about those drugs when they axe, especially if there's no paper trail. One of my best friends from college who got into the Coast Guard warned me to lie about all that shit years ago, but I somehow believed the lie that the Man tells you about knowing everything before the axe you with respect to your past. Well, that's bullshit! If it ain't on paper, they don't know shit, cept' what you tell em'! Enough said about that, I reckon.

It was still spring, but it felt like the autumn of my days at the K-25. I had however been transferred to a new team with a cool supervisor named Bo. My new foreman, an Iron Worker and Mason was a former member of Buckshot Jones's NASCAR pit crew. He played on the company softball team with me and when a lot of others were getting laid-off, made sure that I was kept on during that period. I could not get to sleep at night till it was almost time to leave for work, so I ended up calling in a lot, thus defeating the purpose of staying on I guess. What a lazy ungrateful fucker I was! One softball game, after work, I slid into second base and popped my wrist really hard. That night, a small twister ripped between those two buildings and tore off some of the roof of 33, so none of us got thru the gate that day.

I took the opportunity that morning to go to the doctor and it turned out, I had broken my wrist pretty severely. After that, I was put on the all-time fire watch for the next several months as well as criticality watch for a spell too. The hardest part of that job was staying awake, especially since I was always so tired. And, being on the pain pills in addition to the benzos made me extra sleepy. There was some manager on that site who was a West Point Man and was mostly cool except that he was always trying to sneak up on me to catch me sleeping, but I never let him though.

Work was pretty easy from then on and I didn't miss many shifts at all, for the balance of my stay at K-25. Eventually the last softball game of the season came up and I would always go to watch, even though I was injured. We were one man short so they asked me if I could catch because my arm was almost better. I had a little bit of an ethical dilemma deciding whether or not to play since, I had been assigned such easy work during that time, but I was quickly convinced that it was in the best interests of British Nuclear Fuels if I could go. The defense was good and I got walked three times on twelve straight pitches. Then, in the last inning, the game was on the line, with 2 out, the bases loaded and me up at the plate (and even though, no one thought I should take a swing that night) I surprised everyone by swatting a Texas Leaguer over the shortstop to drive in the winning run! What a rush! I had never helped win a game like that in any sport and it felt great to be a part of something like that.

One day, Congressman Wamp, Senator Frist (the evil one), and then Secretary of Energy, Bill Richardson, who went on to become Governor of New Mexico, came to tour the plant. The Company or DOE thought it would be a good idea for a dog and pony show with us hourly workers to select about 8 union grunts out of about 450 to have lunch with the dignitaries to each table every few minutes, so that they could chat with all of us. Zach barely remembered me and that I had served as his North District Volunteer Coordinator for his initial successful bid for Congress and I wasn't soured against Dr. Frist at that time. Not being too big a fan of Democrats, I was still cordial and respectful when Secretary Richardson sat next to me. I asked him, "what was Bill Clinton like?" and said that I heard he was a pretty nice guy. I then asked him "if Oak Ridge could expect a big announcement of lay-offs within the next few weeks?" So he responded "why did I ask that?" And, I told him that "every time the former Secretary of Energy O'Leary came to town, we always had one soon after her visits." He wouldn't comment on that though, but then, it was his turn to move to another table. He seemed like a pretty good guy for a Democrat and a Delt.

Later that summer, me and my buddy from the Iron Workers went to a big concert at World's Fair Park. This was while I was still living on the waterfront and before we walked over there, we hollowed out a huge Dutch Master's cigar with tweezers and a little screwdriver and filled it full of bud. And, we sneaked it in under my party hat. It looked like a real cigar and not one of those blunts that you slit down the middle to roll. We burned down so hard that night and even managed to get a few women high to boot. Unfortunately, the next day, the boss asked me "if I could pass a drug test?" "Fuck No!" I said, because he had already heard about the night before. He said "well, just do the best you can." There were about seven other workers being tested and I started drinking water immediately. I must have drank about 2 and a half gallons by then, and even tried to talk the pee-collecting dude into leaving a sample for me. He was sympathetic and looked liked a former stoner too, but couldn't do it. So, I peed a few times until it was almost clear. Then, I went out to the water cooler and slammed a couple more cups; after which, I promptly hurled all over the carpeted hallway and even scared some of the people out of their offices. Clean-up on isle one, I guess. The custodian frowned at me as I staggered into the bathroom to give my sample. And, what do you know...it was crystal clear as I handed it to the company nurse. A couple of weeks later, my boss told me that I passed but they (the administration) were extremely suspicious. I'm not sure, but I think me spewing chunks everywhere might have tipped them off a little. Over the next several months, I got tested among every group of 8, randomly of course out of about four hundred and fifty employees, until my untimely exodus from the ETTP later that fall and as far as I know, never failing one.

Despite all the H2O binging and subsequent vomiting, I did manage to get on the ballot that Fall and was humble by virtue that there were quite a few contributions from a wide array of Crafts towards my campaign (for Knoxville City Council) down at the plant. We were trying to buy an airplane pulled ad for a UT football game but, it ended up being too expensive, so I went around and thanked everyone as I returned their money. Given the fact that it was a non-partisan election, those Union Men and Women at K-25 were always very encouraging and supportive of me in spite of my Republican ways and I really appreciated their kindness. They are good folk.

Campaign of '99

Running for Knoxville City Council was a lot of fun that Fall. I was running against a 20 year incumbent who owned a railroad and was certainly a gentleman as well as a community activist who drove a handsome cab horse and buggy. And then there was me, the alcoholic/pill head/stoner dude from the Executive Committee of the County GOP; a veteran political operative with a proven record as a politically incorrect loose cannon. Just ask The Anderson County League of Women Voters?

Buck's Platform: Lets see...

(1) Downtown redevelopment, of course

(2) A Free Party Bus to take revelers between The Strip, Riverfront, and The Old City

  To reduce the number of DUI's

(3) Ease noise restrictions on decibel levels for late night parties on Cumberland Avenue

(4) Also, shut down Cumberland Avenue on one weekend a year for a Drag Racing Festival

I don't remember spending too much cash on this outing, perhaps $52, if that much? The whole campaign was somewhat of a guerilla pr effort. I remember being sober and staying up all night before a UT home football game stapling my posters/flyers up on telephone poles all over Fort Sanders, The Strip and Campus as well as public bulletin boards. I had a decent interview/debate on Politics Knoxville (this was before that outfit betrayed me) as well as co-hosted Late Nite Knox Vegas with my buddies from the UT Track and Cross Country Teams. The Knox Vegas crew was a great bunch of guys and even though they were all super stars, they were humble as hell. I visited and spoke at Republican Clubs across the city and gave interviews to The Sentinel, The Journal, and Daily Beacon.

On Election Day, I was proud to have my Father, Mentor, and a few of my Union Brethren stumping for me at the polls, allowing me to personally visit a lot of different precincts and finish the last few hours at a busy one. That night, when the polls closed, it was a good feeling to see my name on the scroll of the t v screen as the results rolled in. In the end, The Senator and I rode over to the courthouse in his pick-up truck to get the final results. Unfortunately, that night, I came up a little bit short and did not advance to the general election. I was however humbled to receive roughly 2,600 votes or about 17% citywide with a respectable showing at nearly every precinct.

    The day after the election, I was honored that The Vice-Mayor called and asked me to endorse him and the incumbent I ran against. I agreed and wrote a hearty letter to The Editor of The Knoxville New Sentinel in their favor as well as endorsed them on local talk radio and cable access tv and the following City Council meeting.

Hollywood in Sequoyah Hills

During the summer of 2000, when I wasn't saving the environment or mowing lawns, I was engaged in my favorite pastime of partying. I had almost gotten off the Ativans and cut back on the heavy drinking with only an occasional binge.

During that period, I got the opportunity to start hanging out and socializing with one of my best friend's girlfriend over in Sequoyah Hills. She was a socialite and model with a terrific figure and I came to love her but only in platonic way because I had too much respect for my friend to move on his woman. It sounds kind of cheesy, but I really cherished the time we go to spent together that summer.

This was a very happy and carefree time when drugs were just fun and "recreational." At this point, I had no idea what kind of a terribly hellish and surreal nightmare that the next year would bring. My record was clean except for that reckless driving conviction in '91 and I did not worry too much about smoking and driving, especially during the daytime. Even at night, the short drive from Maplehurst down to Neyland Drive and a few blocks West down to Cherokee Boulevard was an inconspicuous breeze, I thought. I was driving an old blue Chevy that Wiser had hooked me up with and it was loud as fuck because I was too trifling to fix the damn muffler. Once you got into her neighborhood, it was like a whole different world; as if you weren't even in Knoxville anymore, but some little rich enclave of nice condos and apartments. They even had their one little gas station as well as an ATM up the street to boot. I reckon a pizza joint, and a dry cleaning business and the filling station selling cold beer would have made it an Eden, especially considering that you could easily have your other party favors conveniently delivered to your door. And, the best thing about this jewel of a community was that nobody would ever fuck with you over there as long as you were relatively well behaved and kept most of the debauchery indoors.

One of the most memorable times I can remember over at Holly's was when we started out drinking beer, smoking swag (but, as I have noted earlier, I could not really even discern too much from common homegrown all the way up to the chronic; they all got me adequately stoned) and listening to tunes. Earlier that day, she and I walked over to the aforementioned ATM up the street and I withdrew eighty bucks to buy supplies with. It was getting late that evening and a lot of folks were calling, but nobody was stopping by. I had never met most of her hip friends and they were hesitant about coming over to party, because they did not know me very well or if I was cool, but only that I was best friends with her old man. They were all just kind of circling in a holding pattern around the neighborhood, until they were adequately satisfied with her vouching for me. Finally, one of them called to ask if he could drop by with his partner. I had never done powder before and was excited about the glamorous history associated with it and was eager to try something different. Since I was a rookie, before anyone got there, she showed me how to lean over and do a hit without hesitating and although that form of it never became my drug of choice, I felt an even more special bond with that woman for sharing the protocol and etiquette with me. That first couple arrived at about 1:30 am. There was a cool amiable black guy and a quite redheaded young woman. They had brought some Natural Lite, so we started in on it. Soon, the coke started coming around and I did my first hit. I felt like this was an important milestone in my drug using life. Although I could not revel too much on this first, because I did not want to reveal my greenness, however in my mind's eye, I felt very chic. Within a few minutes, I rolled a joint and the redheaded gal and I smoked it. It was a small one because I didn't have a lot to start with and although Holly and the man didn't care for any, I thought I had better use it sparingly since it was pretty dry out there. For some reason, I could not seem to get the really good buzz off of the coke that I was expecting, but I did find the synergistic mix of it and the bud to be extremely pleasurable. On the side, I asked Holly if many people smoked pot while they were doing coke and she said that it was not that common but, the ones who did it, really liked it. She indicated that most regular coke people just drank steadily while doing it, in order to balance out the buzz.

After we started partying, more people with more blow started showing up. Despite running out of pot in a few hours, there was plenty of cocaine though. Like I said, I didn't have a lot of the herb, but whatever that I had left, I smoked it with who ever wanted any. Just the way I was raised I reckon, to share that is. Anyhow, before I elected myself the Mayor of Altruism Township, we were out, and nobody on the street seemed to have any either.

As mentioned earlier, I could not really get that rock star buzz feeling off of that stuff which I was hoping and questing for no matter whose stash we were sampling; I thought that I had better follow the plan and keep drinking along with everyone else, which was mostly Bucsh Beer at that hour. And, as I said, I did feel extremely chic about the act of doing powder and the company of whom I was keeping with.

Before daybreak, there were about ten of us sitting around partying and for some reason, I felt like

38

the "guest of honor." Holly had hinted to some of them that I was mostly a "laid back stoner dude" and did not do coke very often. I did feel as though I were being welcomed into a whole new lifestyle, sort of a subculture of Knoxville's ultra-elite, and already I was digging the scene very much (like Hollywood in Sequoyah Hills, I guess!). Soon, we started running low on the suds, so a former UT football player and I were nominated to travel to the beer store when they started selling legally again at around 7am. I was not nearly as drunk as I normally was after partying that long, however I was somewhat bug-eyed. I was actually paranoid about going into a Pilot convenience store on The Strip (which I had been shopping at for years) simply to buy beer and toilet paper. In my mind's eye, I imagined that I would have the beer and toilet paper up at the counter ready to check out and then I would involuntarily start geeking and convulsing. After that, I supposed that the clerk or "manager" would hit a secret button behind the counter, dropping a snare net upon me and within minutes a special SWAT Team from the KPD and Campus Police would arrive to capture me. But seriously, that Vol gave me an encouraging pep talk to help chill me out; and then, I casually walked in and bought the beer and shit paper without incidence, and we were back at the party pad in a few minutes.

It was there, after a long day of partying and in my infinite wisdom, I had decided to stop drinking at midday, which turned out to be a huge mistake physiologically, because I was supposed to keep drinking while I was doing coke! I simply was not following the good and wholesome recommendations of the rest of the milieu.

Around four that afternoon, my head was pounding. I remember shaking and being very hot. I asked a couple of those nearest me, if I seemed to be okay. And the woman, who was sitting just to the left of me, said that she thought I "looked fine." But, I tend to think she was just sucking up to me because I was hooking her up and had also bought her a hit of Ecstasy the week before. And then I remembered, how the weekend before, she had let me know, that it was no big deal that I bought her that hit of E; that other men had bought her plenty before. And I thought, okay...thanks for bringing me up to speed, girl!

One person who did feel my suffering was the black man, the first guest to arrive the night before. He took me into the bathroom and stuck my head under the faucet in the tub with some very cold water because he did not want me to overheat. And I really appreciated that kind of compassion. It was absolutely something like a friend would do for another friend, not just a dealer/customer relationship. After that, he and I went outside thru the garage's entrance into the bright sunlight where we sat on a fence of railroad ties and chatted. Some people went swimming that afternoon and other new folks came and went...but, this was the first time that I had been out of the condo all day since the beer store. I felt like hell and could barely talk, but then an old couple, in a new Cadillac slowly passed by us trying to enter the garage, and I believe my grim face must have been somewhat unsettling to them because they stopped to stare. My new friend quickly urged me to "keep my head up," not just so that I wouldn't scare the neighbors...but "for pride, no matter what," ...and that "everything would be alright."

Later on, I would see him up in the club scene as well as all of the other playas from that night, and it was sort of like we had a secret bond. This was one of the very early twinges of my paranoia about some kind of New World Order Game which I had a delusional thought of one developing all over Knoxville (like Fight Club, I guess .) During this unpleasant experience, I eventually figured out that my physiological sickness was not just a hangover from the abrupt stoppage of drink, but terrible withdrawal symptoms from the benzos which I was in the process of getting off of. Everyone at the condo was vigilantly contacting their various connections to see if one of them could score me some kind of Ativan. Xanax or Valium, but there just weren't any to be found.

Late that afternoon, I can remember being curled up in the far back corner of Holly's storage room where she would come in to check on me every so often. I was even too sick to drive back to my crib. It had been hours, and nobody could find a pill for me, and when she came back to try and comfort me, she exclaimed "I'd just give head for a Xanax (for me) about now." I was still so out of it, I could barely roll over, and I started crawling for the door. Holly laughed and grabbed me and said "no you silly freak," I meant "I was going to get one for you!" Then, I hugged her and told her "I loved her and that that was one of the nicest things a woman had ever offered to do to help me." Despite the rest of my body feeling like complete hell, my heart felt good though knowing I had such a great friend in my corner.

Eventually they took that party on the road to some far out trailer in the sticks. And, after partying there for a while, they were kicked out of there by one of the guy's old lady. After that, the party moved on to some other residences around town and from what I understand, went on for days. Resting up for a few hours, after they had all left, I was able to get up and chug some orange juice from the fridge, and carefully drive back to the apartment at Maplehurst.

Another time that summer, Holly and I partied together when I was able to score some Ecstasy from a mutual friend of ours, who had a reputation for making the good stuff. So that night, it was me, my friend's girl, and that suck up girl mentioned before. I took mine with water, Holly crushed and snorted hers, and the other woman swallowed.

When my buddy snorted hers, she said there were some blueberries in it as well as possibly some heroine.

Anyway, I think this was one of the most psychologically as well as physiologically pleasurably experiences I had ever encountered up to that point in my quest to reach the perfect state of consciousness via various mind altering substances. The pleasurable feelings would just continue to roll thru our bodies as the night went on.

As will be revealed, much later in this text, I would ultimately find that Perfect State of Consciousness; one which was even better than sex, where I could, in my mind's eye and belief actually "Touch the Face of God." And, although this experience of Godhead was many times more intense and pleasurable as the climax of copulation, it was extremely just as brief and came at a much greater cost.

During the course of That Blueberry E Session which I will always remember we each took several more doses to keep it going. By in large though, I guess technically, I only rolled less than a handful of times in my life (not a number dissimilar from the times I had experimented with acid), but I still believe it is one of the best drugs out there for both therapeutic as well as recreational use.

And, just over a year ago, for the first time in ages, I ran into Holly and her son at a hockey game at The Civic Coliseum where I happened to be competing and was subsequently awarded that years coveted title of Mullet King as well as a DVD copy of Joe Dirt with bonus features! What a natural rush that was! (See photos from that night's event.) And, she looked great! I have always loved her as a friend and still wear that friendship ring she gave me back in the day.

It was then getting toward the end of the summer and my focus soon became the upcoming presidential race that fall. These times with the Bush Campaign were a welcomed diversion and delay leading toward the impending doom of the year to follow, however they were intermixed with a couple of strange forays into the fields of block masonry and carpentry.

41

Post-Election Psychedelia

I reckon, after the election until the Connecticut road trip, I started binge drinking again as well as experimenting with acid some. My first experiment with the substance was years earlier and unintentionally. Back in the early nineties, my mentor had chartered a riverboat down in Chattanooga for a private cruise. We had quite a collection of different liquors we had brought aboard and charged a cover for folks to ride and drink plus set-ups. It was a pretty good time for a while. As it turned out though, some wisenheimer prankster had dropped a sheet of acid in the punch bowl and dosed us all! Pretty soon, things got a little weird. The First Mate was down in the engine room in the floor in a fetal position balling like a baby and Captain Pete, who owned the boat, was really pissed. So now, I'm not only drunk as hell (of course, I was already shit-faced when we embarked), but now I was tripping like crazy to boot . Coming out of a blackout, I look up and we're heading down a really narrow channel, plus it looks like we're about to crash into a bridge coming up fast! Being the hero I was, I started running around the boat yelling "we're gonna crash, we're gonna crash,"...until I finally wrestled the steering wheel away from the Captain to save our asses! He was more than a little agitated. That shit really freaked me out.

In the late Fall of '99, some of my neighbors in the Maplehurst community were into acid and offered for me to join them one night. I was not sure and called my iron worker buddy and he advised me to wait because we had to work early the next day, and he told me that he would trip with me soon as a guide, so that I would not freak out. He was always a good friend. And, this was shortly before British Nuclear let me go, but it didn't have anything to do with this trip though.

I think it was a Saturday night when the Vols were off. I was still living in my top floor apartment overlooking the river with my favorite cat Hustler. My buddy had come over and we purchased 4 hits of paper from the neighborhood dealer....Two for my pal and two for me. We needed some weed though, but it was dry and hard to find any that day. So then we ran into some young dudes in the parking lot who were visiting some neighbor I knew in the building and we ended up buying some bud from them.

They didn't want to part with it, but we really needed it and they hooked us up for cheap, which was cool. My friend said "we had everything we needed" and I guess we were ready to begin our journey. The first thing I remember was holding those little squares firmly on my tongue for a while. And, then I remember waking up from being blacked out for what seemed like a couple of hours. I was sweating pretty badly and slinging a lot of snot, so I went and grabbed a bath towel to blow my nose with because I knew it was gonna be a long night. We listened to some music and smoked a bowl about once an hour to take the edge off. When I went to take a leak, it was kind of eerie because I looked in the mirror and it appeared like the skin on my face was melting and that you could really see my skull and eyeballs in a strange way. This went on until about 4 pm the next day and we did not leave the apartment until that time. At this point, my friend and I are still tripping a little, exhausted, but we ended meeting up with LJ and some other old fraternity brother at a nice Mexican restaurant in West Knoxville. I was still a little high, but managed to navigate the bird out there okay. Unfortunately, when we sat down to eat, one of my friend's meals which had already arrived looked remarkably similar to an afterbirth or placenta. And, my using buddy's and my overt commentary on that likeness seemed to clear out the entire dining room with the exception of our table. And, I'm not sure, but I think my friends were a little grossed out too. That first deliberate trip was not necessarily an enjoyable one, but I believe the next one however, enabled me to get a little closer to God though.

Near the end, I did unfortunately shoot myself in the foot one last time with the Laborer's Union. You see, there was a fist fight between the 818 Business Agent and the British Nuclear Fuels Labor Liaison in which the Local's President who was also serving as the Site Steward also jumped in and got banned from the site. After about a month and a half without a steward on site, I took it upon myself to pressure the Local to get us some representation out there (at K-25) and got a petition up to take to the monthly meeting and even went so far as to suggest that member's hold off on paying their dues until the situation was settled. 818 sternly warned me to quit circulating that petition and drop the issue. Naturally, the Local's leadership did not like my rebel- rousing and when I made a duly legal motion during the new business time at the next meeting to get a new steward; the banned President/Former Steward and BA told me that I was out of order and to sit down and shut up. I persisted until they ordered the Sergeant at Arms to escort me out and then about seventeen other men and women walked out with me. Solidarity again, I reckon. I feel bad because most of those folks never worked out of that Local again; however, at the time, I felt like I was doing the right thing for all of us. It just seemed like taxation without representation and all that jazz, I guess. Plus, I tried to instigate a riot out in the street that night in front of the Hall with a 2 x 4 that I had found lying on the curb. After that excommunication, Don Wiser (whom you will hear more about later) was working security for the union that night had calmed me down and told the KPD that he had it under control, when they came to break it up, so fortunately, they left. At the next month's meeting, I went armed with one of those police stinger batons in my boot that another brother had given me in the parking lot. I really wasn't going to take any shit tonight!...I thought. However, once inside, one of my friends who sold pills at the plant and who was an operative of the BA sat in front of me and offered me a couple of purple footballs before the meeting started. And, being the known pill head that I was at the time, I naturally gobbled those Xanax down and not surprisingly, I didn't give a fuck about raising hell at all or any kind of confrontation for that matter all night. It was for the best, but they really hated me after I burned that bridge and I never worked more than a few days as a union member from then on (they even had me blackballed from the Carpenters Union too!) after BNFL let me go that November of '99. I did however get to keep my boots though!

The Generation X Slacker and Spiritual Speculation

I never was much into manual labor... or any kind of labor really for that matter, with the exception of lawn mowing. I guess I started mowing folk's lawns around my last year of junior high or my first year of high school. In the early days, my father would drive me to different yards around the East End of Oak Ridge in his "78 Bronco at first and then when I was allowed to drive, I branched out all over the city. Peculiarly, I had to wait about six months to get my license after the rest of my peers had turned sixteen because my parents were punishing me for calling The 700 Club late one night. This was during the infancy of the 1-900 phone scam days and I reckon it must have cost at least $15 or $20 because my parents freaked out. My God, what kind of a religious fanatic had my Grandparents produced by taking me to Sunday school all those years? And now, I was calling Pat Robertson at 2 in the morning rather than straining my eyes on scrambled Cinemax! Anyway, I guess that is what turned me against Jesus for most of the last half of my life and into a Pagan. Ughh, religion...yuck! Maybe it was this religious incident of a delay in attaining driving privileges and subsequent stunt of growth in social maturity which may have been responsible for my fascination with Anton LaVey's Church of Satan for the last two decades? But now, I am currently worshiping a Masonic Deity known as The Grand Architect of the Universe and even lately started to rediscover Christ. The other day, a beautiful young co-ed from Crown Bible College approached me with some literature while I was trying to get a ticket to the UT basketball game at about 15 minutes till tip-off and let her convert me to Christianity. And, it really didn't take that long either...about 10 minutes I think? She asked me "if I had a personal relationship with Jesus Christ?" And I said " I'm not familiar, does he live around here?"...And then, it was on. She explained everything to me until I got a ticket a few minutes later. I then thanked her for her mission and promised to go visit her at church sometime.

With respect to Christ, it was not that I ever questioned the validity of his ministry or what he did while he was on the planet; it is just that I have a hard time believing that he flew to Heaven (you know, the ascension) or that he even came back to life after he allegedly died on the cross. I hope that lightening does not strike me down and kill or addle me now, for I must surely be spewing blasphemy at this point. However, after that severe beating in Mel Gibson's The Passion of the Christ as well as crucifixion, perhaps he was just in a deep coma in that tomb and they say that that stone was pretty heavy?...Shucks, I digress...I am no religious scholar, nor a man of deep belief except in the existence of a genuine Higher Power. Although, I am recognized as an Ordained Minister with a Doctorate of Divinity commissioned by Dr. Jack Stahl of The Progressive Universal Life Ministries of Sacramento, California (which incidentally was the town where that Bible student was from whom I met at the ball game.) Heck, there was always a standing availability to any of the old crew that I could marry them and their gal for a case of beer. It would of course, had to have been Lowenbrau at that time, and naturally, I would have shared them with everyone at the reception anyway. Hmm..., I was talking about work? Of course, I wasn't much of a worker...ever. I did save enough cash in high school though and my two years at junior college to go on and rush at UT. And, these funds amply financed my training and subsequent addiction as a raging binge alcoholic for the next 20 years. And, I believe that I still have a couple of my original customers from the Disco Era even though I only do a handful a week now during the season, just to stay in shape and put gas in the tank. I guess what it really came down to over the years as to why I never really came into my own with respect to the 9 to 5 clock-punching crowd was because of my damned retiring disposition (that and a rebel-rousing, trouble making mouth that I never could keep from shooting myself in the foot on every decent job that I ever had.) But really, there weren't many good one's over the years and most of them were totally underpaid really sucked.

Yes, back to the retiring disposition...I was really better suited to be a man of leisure; a Jethro Bodine without Uncle Jed's money. The fact that I loved to pick-up and jet-set on any given weekend anywhere from the Bahamas to Martha's Vineyard along with my insatiable appetite for casino gaming were just not adequately funded by my meager mailroom wages. Luckily, during my senior year on The Hill, I had acquired a pair of Visa and Discover Cards to which I gradually maxed out to $ 1,000 a piece. Oh the burden of being on debt row and owing two grand to the system; I was doomed! I did however, eventually pay off the balances to zero over about two years and then it was Party Time! Those credit card apps started coming in fast and furiously. My God...I was pre-approved at nearly two dozen banks at once. Why sure, I didn't hesitate to check that box that I was making $ 60,000 a year! That was all I needed was a handful of Gold Cards from YYZ Bank of So and So with $ 10,000 a piece limits. However, sometimes it was a bitch when the ATM's in Biloxi or Atlantic City would cut you off after five consecutive $200 withdrawals by 5 pm. But, enough of that nasty gambling monkey! Those cards could have kept transferring and increasing for years until I got engaged and had to start paying bills with the damned things and even ended up charging wedding rings on them to boot. I guess the plastic gravy train ended when we reached about 80 thousand. It really sank in and hurt when I had to disconnect the service on that old cinderblock sized Motorola cellular phone for the last time...you just couldn't beat $1 a minute! The Chapter 13 went off without a hitch except that fucker from Sear's was pretty hardcore, but in the end, I fucked them over too and just kept that camping gear we had charged. I had already lost my wedding ring when I was attacked by bees, but that is another tale.

How could I have helped but had a retiring disposition? My Mentor once arranged to have a parapsychologist who was also a past life regression therapist read my past lives and as it turned out, there was a pretty good probability that I was French Aristocracy in a previous life...except that I was a chic and some kind of mistress to boot who ultimately met her demise on the guillotine. Maybe, that's why I lost my head so many times over the years? Or, could it have been the mania? Yes, the Bi-Polar which first reared its ugly head in 1999 after the divorce. A lazy French whore! Maybe, that's why I had always been such a slacker over the years? The seer also saw me as a Civil War soldier who was shot dead in the head. There is a small scar in my forehead (about the size of a .22) which my Mentor points to and it was never clear whether I was a Yankee or a good guy in gray and subsequently, that same nice parapsychologist lady later helped my Mentor exorcise some pretty ugly and menacing demons from my body the night after I nearly fried my brain and overdosed on designer psychedelics, but that is a painful story to recount. And, I certainly appreciate those who helped me survive through it.

But really, the core problem, I believe about me and work was just that I was a lazy fucker! Plus being a hard core binge alcoholic as well as a known pill head with a chronic and persistent mental illness on top of that didn't help much either.

I could itemize my disastrous resume and describe it in all the fucked up minutia of what happened over the years and I more than likely will, but just some at a time. It is far easier to describe the whacked out road trips as well as the sex, drugs, clandestine spy whores, and various hazardous conditions of certain Superfund sites that I showed up for work totally fucked up on some days across this great land of ours. After all, I was trusted by the Government of the United States to deal with radio nuclides as well as asbestos, beryllium and PCB's. And one time, I even worked as a field chemist on an interesting 10 week road trip into the Northeast which involved some international intrigue while being hid away by the FBI.

The Millennium

The new century started like so many other New Year's Eves of the past with me and LJ standing in a bar in the Old City (Hooray's), arms around each other's shoulders, looking at the festivities in NYC and hoping things would be better this year. There was one notable exception at this party in that I don't believe I drank any that night and if I did, it was just one token beer or a highball. The reason for my abstinence was that in a few hours, I was leaving on a road trip at 6 a.m. for work in Connecticut for a few weeks. This was with one of the few temporary agencies that still thought well of me and that I had not burned my bridges with yet. This was a pretty good environmental contractor I was hooked up with. I had spent nearly a week in their shop before we left, assembling electronic components and monitoring equipment that we would need for the trip. We had loaded the truck from a rental company the previous day with everything we needed for the project.

I met the project manager, who was a senior engineer with the company and, on New Year's morning, we left the shop and he drove us strait to Connecticut that day. I remember that they wanted us to drive because if we shipped the equipment by plane, there was a big fear of some terrible meltdown of the transportation grid (for Y2K) and they didn't want to take any chances with the contract. I knew that I would not have to drive that way so I felt comfortable popping a few Ativans for the day so I could zone out. I did drink a lot of coffee that day so I would not pass out in the seat like previously on some drilling trips and was still able to chat coherently with the boss on the drive. It was a long ass drive and the only thing I remember was passing by the West Point exit as well as a brief drive thru tour of the Yale Campus. It was cold as shit when we got there. I do not remember the name of the township where we lodged, but only that it was a few short exits from the Mohican Sun Casino, where incidentally, most of my per diem went. The steam plant we were working at was a bit longer drive away and we worked a lot of hours. I mostly helped the engineers and technicians rig monitoring unit and run wires near the smoke stack and around the rest of the plant.

I had just been diagnosed with bi-polar disorder and was not too familiar with its nuances at that point. I had initially been placed on Lithium but did not take it regularly. I had one joint stashed in my wallet and hinted that I would save it to smoke with a technician when he arrived the second day but, I was a little edgy after dropping two bills at the Reservation that first night and went ahead and smoked it myself. He had been looking forward to it, and was not happy it was gone the next day when he arrived.

I had bad migraines on that trip and was stressing some because the repo man was looking for the Firebird back at home. I called the finance company from the plant one day (using*67), and they were extremely pissed that I was "hiding that vehicle." There was a lot of overtime on that trip and I told them I would make some back payments and get straight with them and I did when I got paid. This gave me a few extra months reprieve before they eventually came and got it. Aside from an interesting trip to Mystic Pizza one night with the guys, not much happened on that job except a lot of work, bitter cold temperatures, and the local Indian Tribe getting a lot of my spending money. I was lucky that I got to fly home after that job, and thankful a couple of other guys drove the shit back to Knoxville. Interestingly, there was a security team, with a contraband sniffing dog patrolling The Hartford International Airport (even pre-9/11) so I was glad I wasn't holding.

Around Independence Day of 2000, I had gotten back on with that same company from the Connecticut trip, for a similar project in Oklahoma. Me and another guy had to drive the stuff down there and he drove the first day and I the rest of the way to Paris, Texas. This time, before we left, I had stocked up on two ounces of really strong bud; the kind with those red hairs in it. I pre-rolled about a dozen doobies with filters with a Joker machine I had purchased, so they looked like regular cigarettes; and I stowed the rest of the dope in my gear, back in the cargo area, with the electronics.

The other fellow and I got there a day before the rest of the crew, so naturally I took the liberty of getting really stoned as fuck that first night and also tossing a couple back in the hotel bar. I had heard about a happening night club from the other patrons, that was "across the highway" from the hotel, so not fearing a DUI, I went exploring. I guess I must have staggered across the road and was out in the median when the cops showed up. There were several cruisers and they used the spotlight; asking me "what the heck was I doing out there wandering around?" I told them "I was looking for that club." "What club" they asked? I did not know and uttered "the one across the highway, I guess." Checking my ID, they wanted to know "what I was doing in town?" I explained about driving the equipment down and that the rest of the company would be there tomorrow. I was honest that I had been drinking in that, I may have appeared a little shit faced, but not about being stoned out of my gourd. I was wearing a navy polo tucked into my jeans and I think they may have given me a break when they saw my Masonic belt buckle because they let me go and walk back to my hotel room which was in sight an only about 200 yards away across a field. I hate ring thumpers, but I don't really think I was doing that with both hands in the air? And, I'm glad that the company did not find out about that little incident or I might have gotten canned before the job even started.

The job site was over an hour's drive into Oklahoma and the work was similar to the Connecticut trip, except this time it was hot as fuck! There were a couple more stacks at this plant and with temperatures being around 105 in the afternoons, we worked at night a lot. Although, we may have worked more at night because the demand for power was lower, I don't know? I guess what I do know is that I stayed fucked up pretty much during this whole trip. If we weren't working, I was smoking, even bringing those faux cigarettes out by the pool in the afternoons. Being the responsible/ safety first dude that I was, I would always quit several hours before we went on, except for one night. I did not want to

49

carry any of that bud back home, so one night towards the end of the job, I rolled a big ole hog leg about as big as a Tijuana Mama Sausage, and major league smoked down. Sadly, I was the only dope smoker on this trip and unfortunately about half way thru it, the boss called the room and said he wanted everybody ready to roll by 3:30 am. This was just too soon!...How was I ever gonna come down by then, so I could safely and professionally perform my job, especially in this state? I had never been so fucked up on a job site in my life; except for maybe that time, I did a little too much GHB on the Defiance Trip, but that is another story. Anyway, it was a little scary, yet exhilarating being several hundred feet up on a windy cat walk, with no fall protection at daybreak. I had always been a sunset man all of my life however, the view up there from so high with me so high too was absolutely incredible with indescribable hues of a pink and azure sky for sunrise that morning.

I did get a chance to check out the local exotic dance scene when I borrowed the company's rented van one night for a visit to the local strip club on the outskirts of town. They had some hot women, but I did not stay long, and the private lap dance I received was mediocre at best. And one night, I actually drove somewhere down the road to a private establishment called The Longhorn Club which was a pretty strange joint. But then again, I was a pretty strange character. All this, while so extremely stoned, I guess it was truly a semi-charmed life, at that point at least. I am just glad there was no casino close by that trip, although I did pitch a fit because my partner would not allow us to stop in Tunica on the way home. I reckon he was too good of a company man for that type of shenanigans and probably eager to get back to his wife to boot. Needless to say, I never worked for that contractor again, either.

The Overdose

After I got back from Connecticut, not only did I save the Firebird for a little while longer, but I even had more money to party with in addition to my unemployment checks. I was in the process of moving from the riverfront apartment to one up the hill across from Neyland Hills Apartments, because they wanted to tear down my old place so Game Day of Auburn (Alabama) could build some fancy condos for the rich. Just another reason to hate that state I guess. So when I really wanted to blow it out, I always walked or got a ride to The Strip , so that I would not jeopardize the car or my license.

Down the road, there was a commune/think tank in the neighborhood and I smoked weed with it members occasionally. That organization's Founder was a brilliant man and his beautiful young partner was both intelligent and sweet. I recall them both being bi and cool. Anyway, that spring, one of their gay friends and chemistry major, came up with an interesting designer psychedelic. I believe it was made out of some furniture factory varnish as a precursor. I don't remember what it was called, but it had a one letter name that it was known as and had some effects similar to ecstasy except that it was a lot harsher at higher doses. It was relatively inexpensive and I took one capsule, one night before I went out to a dance club (The Old Library or U Club) on Cumberland Avenue. Everything felt really good and the spinning lights of the club looked extra freaky. The next weekend, I took two doses and just hung out at the commune where his girlfriend and I rubbed Vick's Vapor Rub on each other's hands in a platonic yet extremely pleasant and tactile experience.

The following weekend, the others took three, but stayed at the commune in a safe and controlled environment. I however, had plans to go to a private party at an old club on The Strip that my buddies from the track team had rented to celebrate the end of the Dogwood Relays. This was mostly a beer bash style party and I made one of the biggest mistakes of my life when I intentionally took four of those capsules instead of three. I was foolishly convinced that this stuff was just like ecstasy (which I really had little experience with either) from my earlier doses. In hindsight, I guess even four hits of E would have been too much too.

Pretty soon, I was sweating like crazy, trying to walk around and chat with people but, I was tweaking so hard that I was shaking and twitching as I walked like some out of control Frankenstein or robot. It was a near total loss of motor skills because my body would not respond to my brain's impulses or commands to walk normal. I do not know if I was more embarrassed to be so fucked up and out of control in front of my friends because I was sure they all knew what I had done to myself (I had told a lot of them what I was on anyway) or more concerned with the fact that I was actually in the process of an overdose from which I could easily fry my brain or die. And, even worse than my own embarrassment, I knew that those that those bunch of kids were embarrassed for me too, especially in front of their out of town guests who were track and field athletes also. Plus, I even hooked some other friends up with that evil shit that night. They had come to the club to pick up a few capsules for a house party they were going to, and even they were concerned about me being so fucked up and had offered to take me home. I unfortunately, being as hardheaded as I was, was determined to stay and to return back to normal in order to redeem myself in front of the other partygoers (when the smart thing to do would have been to get my ass to an emergency room.) I even had a small jar of Vick's Vapor Rub and one of those Vic's inhalers that partiers use to blow on each other's faces and there was one dude who was talking to me who said "yeah, you're a real rolling motherfucker." What an uncompassionate smartass! Anyway, I had not drunk for a month or so, but I knew that I had to do something in a hurry to come down or I would become a vegetable. There was not a downer in the whole joint, so I asked one of the guys at the pool table for his pitcher of beer. I sat down on the table and chugged it all and then bought one from the bar and chugged it too, strait out of the pitcher. This helped a little and had the sedating effect I had hoped for. After the club closed, I ended up at that same house (where the track guys lived) from that meth/rock concert weekend. The guys and girls from the track and cross country teams looked after me until I came down and was in the clear, which I appreciated. And, then, I did some runner's stretches and jogged home at about 4 am. As for my track buddies, I unfortunately burned my bridges with this crew too, by getting out of control (I never in my life imagined that I would OD on something, but it happened and I was lucky enough to live, have my wits, and tell about it) and I did not see them much until a Halloween party at a well known acid house in Maplehurst that Fall.

Kentucky Derby Tales

They say insanity is repeating the same thing but expecting a different result. Well, a few weeks after I nearly killed myself with that overdose, I took a couple of those same capsules with me to Louisville, Kentucky for the Derby. But only 2, which was two too many, because I shacked and twitched like a zombie all afternoon in front of my old college buddies as well as the rest of the infield. I could barely place my bets; I was trembling so hard and it seemed like everyone was staring at me. I drank plenty though after that, and lived again, but would not return to Church Hill Downs for four more years. Later, at that time in 2004, I was 3 months in recovery from alcohol; however, I had just received a large back payment from the government, and was secretly in the early stages of one of the most ugly and difficult addictions known to man, at least of the last quarter century.

Now back to the happier days with just one addiction at the time known as chronic binge alcoholism. Tony, Holmes, and I started going to the Derby (Infield) for well over a decade continuously (but only Holmes knows the exact number of years) and each year we learned a new trick for a better trip. For many years, we would take a gallon of Jim Beam and transfer it to half of our small plastic Coke bottles (carefully without breaking the seals) mixed with Coke and then we would refill the gallon bottle with water and Coke to look like whiskey. The Coke/liquor bottles would go on the bottom of the cooler under ice with the plain Cokes for mixers; and on top we would put the gallon of Beam decoy under a little ice on top. At the infield entrance, when they opened our cooler to search, the first thing they uncovered was that fake bottle of Beam. They held it up so high to show their fellow staff as well as the other race fans (look how stupid these fuckers are) and we would just shake our heads in fake disgust (as if, damn I can't believe we got busted). After that, they would just rustle around the real mixed bottles and close the top and wave us on thru. By the time we got in the tunnel, we were laughing like hell because we had just fucked them again. This little ruse worked well for about 8 years until one fateful first Saturday of May. One time, after paying our infield fee (which was more and more every year) LJ, who was with us on this trip, and I were carrying a large cooler and we ended up going on opposite sides of a steel pole! As would happen, the ice box busted open, spilling everything on the ground and our whole cache of liquor was confiscated that year. And subsequently, we ended up having to buy those weak $7.50 mint juleps and tepid $6 beers all day. I always liked to drink the local drink wherever I was though. If I was in the Bahamas, it was the Bahamas Mama...Cape Cod, ect. But the juleps at The Downs weren't that good. I suppose that they were mass mixed by amateurs or perhaps once a year greenhorn bartenders; but I reckon they did the best they could.

I guess one of the most memorable or at least semi-lucid Derbies was one by a horse named Go for Gin. Being a superstitious drunk, every year before I got too hammered, I always placed a twenty at the start of the day on any Derby horse with an alcohol reference in its name to win. And, it just so happened that I got exceptionally sloshed on that extremely rainy and muddy day at The Downs (which was not unusual for me at the Derby) and when my horse won, I knew the payoff would be sweet. So, on the way to the window to collect with my friend and former Pledge Educator (who saved my ass in Athens that time) escorting me again, I got a little sidetracked into some impromptu infield mud wrestling. There was a busty blonde covered in mud who challenged me to jump into their pit. Well, being the redneck playboy that I was, I dove right in and started wrastlin like crazy. The crowd of hundreds started growing bigger and the overhead camera on a cable from CBS Sports came over so we thought that we should give the fans a good show. We were slipperier than 2 eels in oil and just laughing and having fun, but it turned out that she had a jealous boyfriend. So, I had the woman pinned and we were both still laughing and then, her old man was getting ready to punch me in the back of the head. My Pledge Ed had my back though and told the guy that he better stop right there if he knew what was good for him. The match ended right after that and I hugged the girl and the crowd cheered.

Believe it or not, that winning ticket was not in very good shape after being subjected to all that mud and water. So, my friend and I waited in line and when we got up there, this mean and chunky girl said "I can't take this ticket." "What do you mean?...It's a winner" I exclaimed! "The computer can't read it like this, it's invalid" she quipped. This was a lot of money for me at the time and would have helped subsidize that trip significantly. "Invalid my Ass!" I shouted as I reached under the cage to grab my ticket and yelled "Oh you'll pay!" And then, my buddy grabbed me and pulled me back before she started to yell for the cops. Anyway, she came out and we filled out some "official" claim form and she said that the "Down's Financial Office" would mail me a check in a few weeks. Well, that fat bitch lied and this time I got rolled while I was still awake! I called up there several times (long distance) from work over the next couple of months and they said that they had never heard of her or even had any record of that form. I guess she probably cashed that ticket in in herself; so she and her bovine buddies must have partied big that night on my winnings. After that, I decided the next year I would use a zip-lock bag to hold my tickets of drink less; more likely the former than the latter. Unfortunately, I never hit another big winner like that over the years again. But, to add insult to injury, after the 9th race I had passed out at our encampment and got rolled again! This time they took my Teva's...Dirty rogue bastards! I had to walk all the way out there as well as ride the bus back barefooted. Once again, my mind pondered the question of whether I might have some sort of a drinking problem? I guess, I didn't get so fucked up the next year, however, from college on and during those days, instead of focusing on a career or steady job like most guys my age; I was still following a hopeful (or was it a hopeless?) quest of finding the ultimate party. How fucking Nobel I was?...but ultimately, in time, I was able to narrow my search down to finding the ultimate high via drugs.

Sex and The Census

Another job I had back in 2000 was working for the United States Census Bureau. Wow, me a trusted quasi civil servant? That is almost as fucked up as when the government certified me to work in nuclear plants and around radioactive waste. The job was very short lived though. The training lasted a few days and went alright, but most of my assignments were in the projects of East Knoxville. These people really didn't want you in their homes to interview them especially if they were selected for the long form. So, a lot of times I just made shit up, and filled out the forms for them, especially when they were ugly to me. There was however, one young woman who was a student at the Tennessee School of Beauty who was flirting with me, so I casually asked her out. She said "no" and I was friendly and said "thanks anyway" and left. Then, the next day the supervisor fired me because the woman's mom complained to the government that I was stalking her under aged daughter....Under aged? I figured, if she was a student at TSB, she was at least out of high school and was college aged. If she was that young, she should not have been hitting on me. What the real problem was a Census worker up North had allegedly beat up and raped an interviewee the day before. The national media had caught on to that violent crime and I guess those ghetto rats thought I was part of some nationwide sex conspiracy. And, I reckon my discharge was just a typical government kneejerk reaction since some people have a tendency to be so litigious and the man didn't want to risk a potentially expensive law suit. I'm sure they could have made a bundle.

So, to make a long story short, the pay sucked and the people were not very cooperative with the information anyway (even though a lot of these figures were taken especially to justify benefiting those areas in the long run, with more government money) and I did not give a shit about losing that temporary job. I did however, not want anyone to think I was some kind of predator or perv, so I didn't make too much of a big deal and just left without incident and did not show my ass (for once).

I don't recommend that type of work for anyone in the future though because it is a hassle and more trouble than it is worth. Who knows, in the future, maybe they will have little government robots that can go around the hood, passing out free rocks or blunts to butter people up into giving out that kind of personal baby daddy info. But then again, the robot would probably get jacked or rolled.

The Rise and Fall of 2000

The Rise and FALL of 2000: Although I had worked on a variety of local and federal campaigns during the nineties, Governor and now President Bush's successful bid for the White House in 2000 was one of the most fun runs that I ever participated in.

It was a very hot day in August of that year when Senator Burchett and I first arrived at the new headquarters on Kingston Pike to help Mrs. Chedester hang the massive Bush/Cheney 2000 banner from the roof. Things had been running along pretty smoothly with respect to finances and mental health despite my recent self-diagnosis with Bi-Polar Disorder (out of DSM III) in the fall of 1999. Although I was still receiving partial unemployment checks from when I had lost my job at British Nuclear Fuels Ltd for failing to get a clearance (because I had admitted to experimenting with pot in college and inhaling), there was not enough money to hold onto the Firebird and it was repossessed. It is kind of funny but, even after all these years, some jackass Yankee law firm keeps calling me to find out when I'm gonna pay them that $2,500 which I was upside down on it? The only thing was that, when I kept asking him about some specific details relating to this conundrum, this curt, dumb fuck couldn't even answer any of my questions about this account! But oddly enough though and thru all of his stupidity and cluelessness, he still maintained that fast talking Yankee dick headed diction and tone which a fellow can really only take so much of...so I just hung up on his sorry ass.

As far as the campaign building up to The Presidential Election of 2000, about a month into it, I was already drinking again. And, quite frankly I might add nearly every night even though historically, I had primarily been a binge drinker over the years. Things had become really tight monetarily, so maintenance as well as insurance covering the old blue Chevy naturally fell by the wayside. Rent really didn't seem all that too important a concern either along with the intermittent service provided by the local utilities and telephone companies. I was however, still able to maintain a nice collection of ballistic nylon weapons as well as assorted rifles, a handy but sturdy post-ban Uzi sub machine gun, and a nifty little 12 gauge shotgun which, I believe, in its riot configuration, might have been just barely legal.

As I have said, that old blue beast of a car was noisy as hell and it was all I could do just to keep gas in it because it seemed to burn right thru it, real quickly. Upon rudimentary inspection, I noticed that that filthy ole muffler was worn out and rusted so bad that afro-engineering it with chicken wire, duct tape, and coat hangers never seemed to last too long either. Sometimes, it concerned me when friends told me how flames would shoot out of the hole in the muffler where the tailpipe previously existed; however being back off of the Ativan wagon, the more of them I ate, the less these potentially little catastrophic conditions in need of attention seemed to matter, even those prickly little wires and marble sized bulges protruding from the tires. With respect to those flames, I'm not sure if the cause might have been fuel spurting out of those holes in the muffler, the sparks from where it sometimes dragged the pavement or a combination of both of these pesky conditions, but I did not find generic super glue to be all that successful in remedying this problem either. I reckon, I should have splurged a few more cents for the name brand glue, especially considering I was already using that expensive metal thousand mile an hour tape that they use on jets to patch my muffler with. Basically it was a very sick car, as some of my friends noted, especially with the ungodly noisiness. They would say that you could hear me coming from a mile away when I used to roll up upon The W Headquarters nearly every afternoon. Usually I would head for the back room to scarf down a slice of cold pizza or some stale pretzels and wash it down with some artificially flavored fruit punch before work. Then I would hit the can for a quick hobo shower in the bathroom sink before I hit the floor. Having picked up a new campaign tee on the way into the head, after freshening up, I would tuck it into my britches and pop in some Dentyne Ice on my way to the call center as I was preparing to do some serious politicking. Next, I would pick up a clipboard, snap on a Bush/Cheney button and stroll around the facility making sure that all of the co-ed volunteers from the sororities on campus were able to understand the complicated nuances of our elaborate, state-of-the-art phone bank system and, when needed, train them accordingly. A lot of times, I would have to spend a little more time with The Freshmen and sophomores since this was usually the first time that they had worked on a campaign, more less even voted. But, I didn't mind too much; heck, I'd have done almost anything for my party. And besides, since my humble years of service to The Young Republicans were winding down; it was only natural for a good party man like me to offer his wholesome mentorship to one of our fine associated bodies such as The College Republicans. Sometimes, I would even make an actual call or two to a potential voter just so they could experience the rush of watching a real life hardcore political operative in action. Most of the time (for example purposes only), I would just make the same stock call to a certain former State Representative's home; however I don't believe that he wholeheartedly embraced our obligation as Republican leaders to properly usher in and conservatively mold and educate our next generation of The GOP, at least, not as seriously as I had. Unfortunately, after his brief stint in government, I guess he was a little soured from all of the injustices which exist in modern politics. I have to say that I felt his angst against the system such as the one that I felt towards U.S. Congressman Zach Wamp after his successful bid, back in the day. After busting my ass so hard for nearly 2 years as his North District Volunteer Coordinator, I expected to be rewarded with one of those prestigious jobs as a staffer in DC or one of the district offices, but was not.

But, volunteering for W was great, with no expectations. Occasionally, Mrs. Chedester would help me with a few dollars to square my beer tab at Sonny's, but I felt a little guilty asking a fine upstanding Christian woman like herself to subsidize my unsavory drinking habit.

It was a few weeks after I had started volunteering at The Bush headquarters with Stacey Campfield (now a State Senator) and Tyler Harber (of Knoxville's GOP Gate,) and had gotten on with a block layer over in Oak Ridge who was cousins with my Iron Worker buddy. He was one of the toughest and baddest men that I had ever met, and told me that I could refer to him as cousin too.

I believe that my new tough guy image came from the three weeks that I was working as a block laborer and had gotten extremely bulked and buffed with perhaps even a little extra testosterone in addition to the increased self confidence. And, I reckon, under Mrs. Chedester's and Billy Stoke's(who is currently running for Judge) guidance, I did a decent job as the "Facilities Manager" for the headquarters. At least that seemed like an accurate title and description of what I considered myself to be contributing during this campaign. I would do whatever was needed. As previously noted, I would train phone bank workers as well as occasionally make a few calls myself. I would work up front greeting and receiving visitors, horse trade with other county parties for supplies with yard signs, campaign buttons, bumper stickers and tee-shirts. One time, Mrs. Chedester gave me some money to purchase some pumpkins and bales of hay from the local farmer's market for decorating out in front of the HQ for Halloween.

And then, one of my favorite stunts as a political operative was the morning before the UT/Alabama home football game. At about 4 am that Saturday, I walked out to the middle of the train trestle and hung a huge Bush/Cheney 2000 banner over the side of the bridge. It was about as big as a piece of paneling and I had another on in the crib covering the front window. This kept out a lot of bright light and was nice for privacy considering how paranoid I was becoming. Anyway, I checked up on the status of my little publicity stunt at about 10 am and apparently some dirty Democrat, or a sorry Democratic sympathizer had cut one of the stabilizer lines; so I walked out there again and restrung it. It was dangerous and I almost fell off, slipping on that loose gravel out there, but being the perfectionist that I am, it had to be straight and balanced. Despite being a little edgy out there, some drunks from The Boathouse Restaurant below were either cheering me on for my party loyalty or rather encouraging me to jump. From my vantage point and distance earshot however, their shouts were indistinctively subjective and one could speculate that the leanings of their urgings depended largely on their party affiliation. Happily, I believe that the sign did manage to stay up during the majority of the game, because it looked pretty good from the top of the South Ramp, mid-way through the 3rd quarter. And, most importantly, the whole stunt got a lot of exposure for W, which was exactly what I had intended; Guerilla PR, you know.

One particular incident at the HQ that I found particularly amusing: there was this big pansy, a pompous jackass from some West Knoxville Neighborhood Association who used to occasionally pop in down there, mostly just to bitch and whine about the way thing were being run. I remember one day in Mrs. Chedester's office, I was sitting to his left and Jane to his right. So I'm trying to get his attention while he was blowing all this inane hot air and I lightly nudge his knee with my shoe. And, this huge gaping vagina freaks out and screams like a little bitch to Jane that I had kicked him! So, I said "I didn't kick you, I nudged you, if I had wanted to kick you, I'd have fucked you up really bad!" Anyway, he demanded to Ms. Jane to have me thrown out of the headquarters, because "I was just a common thug." He even called my friend Tim to complain about how I had terrorized him. What a wuss! And finally, after he had harassed Ms. Jane to inform Party Chairman Billy Stokes (a burley, Harley riding, attorney, who supervised the headquarters) about the incident. I heard Billy (who years later, had initiated into the 32nd degree of The Scottish Rite, in the same class as me) had just laughed about the incident. And, to this day, I always thought real well of him.

And, also to this day, that malcontent is still writing his whiney little letters to the Editor's complaining about The Supreme Court and how its liberal judges did too much legislating from the bench. Get a life, you loser!

Let's see, I remember when then Governor Bush was scheduled to appear at Doyle Middle School in South Knoxville on The Barnstorming with Bush Tour. At the Headquarters, we had a limited number of regular tickets and an even smaller number of VIP passes. And, there was a huge demand among local Republicans wanting to attend this exclusive event. It had been a while, but as usual, in a situation like this I thought it might be a good time to break out the old counterfeiting kit and fire up The Cochran Press one more time. With my obsessive perfectionism being at the very heart of this artistic medium, in my arrogant redneck opinion, I believe I had turned out some very decent replicas of the VIP passes for 20 of my closest friends...and, they didn't even have to waste any time filling out those cumbersome Secret Service background forms either. Of course this was pre/911 and War on Terror with all of those heightened security measures had not fully kicked into gear yet. And, as a matter of fact, future First Lady Laura Bush even took the time to autograph one of those fake passes which I had crafted...I was so proud and eventually ended up giving it to my mother to display with her autograph collection, since she is a big fan of The First Ladies (with the exception of Hillary, of course.)

It was really a nice set-up, out there at the school, probably the norm I guess, for serious journalists like myself. I had checked in earlier that day and went ahead and registered as a special correspondent with Politics Knoxville. They had some pretty good food in there once you got past the metal detector and armed guards. There was especially a lot of fresh fruit in the lunch room, plus about 30 telephones were available and as long as you had your "credentials," you could make free telephone calls to almost anywhere in the world, but mostly to you bureaus or editors or whoever else you fucking wanted to call, even your old pals from college.

Outside, I made friends with some of the Secret Service guys who were manning the security portal at the main entrance, and as it turned out, one of them was a fellow Mason, from a Lodge in Arlington, Virginia. It really makes you feel proud, that upright and dedicated brothers like this man were providing security for the future President of The United States and his First Lady! Although I went in and out of the facility as often as I pleased, it was difficult not to feel sorry for the folks in an extremely long line with genuine tickets waiting patiently for admittance as well as those hoping to obtain tickets to get in also, because most of them were never even gonna get close. And, that line snaked all the way across campus, up the main access road and nearly completely off of the school grounds. I had heard that the campaign had set up a remote viewing site nearby under a tent on the athletic field to accommodate a potential overflow crowd, but I didn't see any tents though.

Being about an hour till the speech was scheduled I decided to walk the length of the line to chat with some of the other good Republicans. As I walked the line, I ran into some folks from that crappy job with Cobble Personnel which I suffered thru during the early days of The Clinton Administration a few years after college, when the economy was so robust. I guess the only good thing about those three shitty years at International Harvester was that I was able to more finely hone my counterfeiting skills after my brief stint at Boeing (more great economic times, that I think the Media referred to as a recession) where I first realized that I had a knack for forging bogus credentials. But, as I have said so many times, even when the work sucked, it was the people or fellow sufferers which I felt akin and somewhat of a camaraderie with. So as much as I appreciated friendly former co-workers, I gladly hooked them up with some VIP tickets as well as passing out a few more of them to some very conservative, yet seemingly repressed nice looking young women from the Bible College. And, I even parted with a couple more to some sexy MILFs with their rug-rats in tow. Wow, what an awesome fucking humanitarian I was back in those days, and a moderate, yet loyal party man to boot. I did feel a little bad though for several folks who really wanted in and even offered me a hundred dollars apiece for my credentials to get up close. That would just not have been ethical, especially since they only cost me a couple of dollars to make in the first place. But, more importantly, even though it was pre/911 I couldn't have possibly vouched for these wanna be customers to my brothers in arms with The United States Secret Service, so I just ended up eating my extras. Besides, if I had unscrupulously sold these people a ticket(s), they might have been some kind of dirty Democrat interlopers, who would have thought they had bought themselves a license to get in there and heckle the Governor, and you know, they are like that. I've seen it before at a few events, with their childish antics: they have absolutely no respect for decorum. I did not want to take any kind of chance on our man being distracted that day (because, he never was that good at delivering a speech to start with) especially the way the leftist mainstream media had been dogging him everywhere he went, day in and day out, to desperately try and manipulate the election in favor of Gore/Loserman.

As my hike continued, the farther back the line got towards the Carpenters Union Training Center and the main road, the more liberal and radical they became. This last 30 yards up that hill was a hotbed area of ultra liberal protesters including the stupid dregs from the Carpenters Union, a handful of gay and lesbians, and even some evil bitches from the local Libertarian Party were there. And they (the Libertarians) disliked me almost as much as the Carpenters because they said at meetings I babbled like a crazy man after I smoked down with them and made them feel uncomfortable. Well, boo fuckin hoo!...So, I was manic with the bi-polar and weed made me chatty. Yeah, I could carry on a pretty spirited conversation with myself when I was stoned, but I certainly didn't need some phony baloney, fake intellectual, hippie whore pointing out my flaws and trying to salt my game at a political rally. This pathetic band of malcontents was not only unsightly and pesky, but emotionally mean spirited as hell. It was quite a spectacle how they then, as always seem to make asses of themselves whenever a Republican leader comes to town. It was that way when Reagan came to campus at UT back in '85 and then a few years later when Bush Sr. visited The Hill.

Although, there's nothing more exciting to a political junkie than being in that gym for the speech itself, it was actual hot as fuck in there and ultimately, those people listening to it outside were probably a lot more comfortable anyway.

About a month earlier, Mrs. Chedester had helped me get some money raised by selling special Bush campaign buttons, of which I foolishly used as an initiation fee for this rogue Carpenter's Union scam which was going on during this period. It was expensive too, maybe around $150.00 at the time, if not more. Also, I aced their placement test, so Doug The Trainer said he would start me out as a "second year apprentice." Big Fuckin Deal! That jackass jumped my case the day of that speech for being a "traitor to the union" and told me to never come back. This was also after I had put in 2 days of free labor (or training,) installing a new ceiling in their sorry ass Carpenter's Union Hall downtown. And, a for a few weeks , the late Kenny McCormic ,their Business Agent ran me out of their business office too, when I showed up looking for work. So then, this arrogant redneck keeps every bit of my initiation fee and dues as well. Maybe The DA could Crack the case on this corrupt outfit?

Anyway, after dealing with all of those ultra-left wing losers, I made my way back down to the gymnasium for the Governor's speech. The only bad thing was, when I got back there, all the VIP space was full. I guess I fucked around a little too much out front or perhaps may have even made too many passes for such a small venue. I really wanted to meet Governor Bush, but he was exiting to the far left side of the gym and I was stuck on the right. This was, however, where I was able to procure the future First Lady's autograph.

Naturally, I was somewhat bummed out because I wanted to meet our next President. I did however hear that he was scheduled to make a brief appearance at Congressman Jimmy Duncan's Family Barbeque that night at the Civic Coliseum. So I decided to attend, and after his speech, I headed to stage right, similar to the path he had taken earlier in the day leaving the school gym. Although he was heavily guarded as he walked by, I reached over a couple of people in front of me with my long arm to shake hands with him and said, "Hey Governor, we really appreciate you coming to see us over here in Tennessee!" And, he replied "Well, thank you...we'll be coming back before the election." So then, having accomplished my aim, I took off. They say, it's hard to get a handshake like that, especially with a nominee in these times of heightened security. I guess I'm thankful to have been recognized as an upright and trusted GOP Operative at that point before all that 9/11 hysteria took over.

And, The Mainstream Media Projects...No Wait, We Take That Back

The Florida Fiasco and The Cluster Fuck of The Hanging Chad:

Election Night that November was a little strange, to say the least. From our top floor vantage point at the Crown Plaza (GOP Suite) downtown, we hardcore operatives could tell that there was trouble with the votes as we were looking towards the South at the old courthouse. There were a whole lot more blue lights flashing over there that night than usual.

My arrogant redneck speculation at that point was that the lady in charge over there at the Election Commission (a Democrat) had held back on releasing some vote totals and information in an attempt to influence the undecided elections still in progress in California and also effect the fiasco in Florida. In response to this official's alleged games on election night, The Senator (Tim Burchett) held a forum at The City/County Building about her actions a month after that. This allowed guys like me the opportunity to take the podium and just rail on her Democrat bias, which ultimately manipulated public opinion enough to get her run out of office.

So on election night, I started out drinking at a moderate clip because we were looking for a big win and everyone was in a celebratory partying mood with the exception of that far right ultra-conservative faction which doesn't drink anyway. Anyway they were probably mostly staying in that night so that they could hold a constant prayer vigil for a Bush win or preparing those lessons for mom to home school the children, the next day. Shortly, as the major networks started taking back states like Florida from red to blue or green or whatever; most of us (even myself) put away the drink and started sobering up pretty quick. What kind of a Godless left wing conspiracy were these sore losers from the mainstream media trying to pull?

There was so much good camaraderie during that campaign and it felt like we were really doing something important as a tight knit team to help W win the White House that year. Who would have thought, all these years later, he would have started such a senseless war in the Middle East just to line the pockets of his and the Vice-President's war profiteering cronies like Halliburton. And now that he has purposefully extended this silly conflict to over four years, when it could have been wrapped up in 2 weeks, he has not only screwed over the folks who fought so hard to get him in there...by losing The Congress and Senate for us Republicans, but now he is trying to give The Democrats The White House

63

too, on his way back to Texas. We had so much pride and hope for the future at those rallies at the school and the Coliseum as well as that entire Fall...and it is sad how W the War Monger has betrayed all of his loyal followers (except perhaps to those within The New World Order Movement and I reckon that he is probably just a slave to their mastery.)

After midnight, my head started pounding from the abrupt alcohol stoppage. I was also, unfortunately, turning extremely manic as a handful of us die-hard campaigners holed up at the suite until about 2:30 or 3am trying to disseminate the fucked up numbers from that night. If I could just find a way to chill out and get some rest, surely this thing would be decided in a few hours by the time the morning news cycles had begun? At that point, we could hardly imagine that all of that fucked up shit would go on for nearly a month before the Supreme Court would have to decide this this thing. Being near exhaustion, I hauled my rangy ass on back to the apartment by the riverfront. Naturally, I could not sleep worth a damn, tossing and turning until daybreak, when the mainstream media were still trying to stir up shit and declare Gore victorious. And, for some fucked up reason (and my infamous one man gang activist attitude,) I had decided that I would post-up on the foot bridge on campus crossing Cumberland in front of Strong Hall, proudly holding up a Bush/Cheney sign at about 9 am. Not surprisingly, the response was mixed. The Police, Firefighters, and EMTs and other conservatives threw their thumbs up and honked in support; while some black cafeteria workers from Sophie's came out and cussed me. There were even some red-necks, in their Nissan pick-up passing underneath who really showed their asses by throwing rocks and small denomination coins at me. I was just trying to let people know that us Republicans were in for the long haul. I took a short break at mid-day to run out and see what was up at the headquarters and ended up giving an interview for the TV news that night. The reporter was one of my favorite news babes at the time, but she had to stop the interview and begin it a second time because she wanted me to look at her and not into the camera.

The message was simple: just that "we were tired," but planned to keep up the fight for a long as necessary!

Then, I headed back over to campus to close out my mission at the bridge until 5, because it was getting cold and dark.

Looking back, I wish I had gone down to Florida with all of those other hell raising GOP operatives, but the coffer was running a little thin. And, I reckon I missed out on a once in a lifetime experience, not unlike the '86 Sugar Bowl when my closest friends travelled down to New Orleans to witness Tennessee whip the shit out of Testeverde and The Canes and (from what I understood) enjoy one of the greatest partying road trips of the late 20th Century.

It took a while that fall, but ultimately The GOP won+ and The Sore/Loserman Team lost and they've never gotten over it!

And, The Democrats are still bitching, that if only convicted felons would have been allowed to vote in Florida, they would have won it all? Whaaah!

As I've said. in 2000, we had a very tight group of operatives. I got to be pretty good friends with Sen. Campfield (from the Lincoln Day Ordeal) as well as fellow operative Tyler Harber (of Knoxville's GOP Gate,) Mrs. Chedester from the headquarters who was really good to all of us as the Matriarch of our campaign and her daughter (who had recently been crowned Miss Knoxville in that year's Pageant,) was smoking hot; however, I found her terse e-mail to my best friend to be extremely unimpressive.

The old crew from the HQ did get a chance to meet one final time up at Jack Barne's Christmas Party at The Kerbela Shrine across the river. Mrs. Chedester (whose aforementioned daughter sang a patriotic song that day,) was pleased to see all of us together again, but it was a bittersweet reunion. Bush/2000 was a special time in our lives because of all of the good chemistry, synergy, and camaraderie. And I was sad that it was over.

END 2000

Buck Cochran holds a Bachelor's of Science in Business Administration from The University of Tennessee's Glocker School of Business. He earned Certificates of Diploma in Industrial Hygiene and Waste Management in the field of Environmental Health Technology from Roane State College where he finished Magna Cum Laude. Cochran is the Co-Founder of The Da Vinci Institute for Socio-Political Thought AKA The PGT Consulting Group with Dr. Gary Coleman. He currently resides in The Historic City of North Knoxville.